A JOURNEY
Beyond
A JOURNEY

A Journey Beyond A Journey

Leaving It All Behind
&
Finding That Mustard Seed Within

Ayoka Brown

Xulon Press

Xulon Press
555 Winderley Pl, Suite 225
Maitland, FL 32751
407.339.4217
www.xulonpress.com

© 2023 by Ayoka Brown

All rights reserved solely by the author. The author guarantees all contents are original and do not infringe upon the legal rights of any other person or work. No part of this book may be reproduced in any form without the permission of the author.

Due to the changing nature of the Internet, if there are any web addresses, links, or URLs included in this manuscript, these may have been altered and may no longer be accessible. The views and opinions shared in this book belong solely to the author and do not necessarily reflect those of the publisher. The publisher therefore disclaims responsibility for the views or opinions expressed within the work.

Unless otherwise indicated, Scripture quotations taken from the New American Standard Bible (NASB). Copyright © 1960, 1962, 1963, 1968, 1971, 1972, 1973, 1975, 1977, 1995 by The Lockman Foundation. Used by permission. All rights reserved.

Scripture quotations taken from the Amplified Bible (AMP). Copyright © 1954, 1958, 1962, 1964, 1965, 1987 by The Lockman Foundation. Used by permission. All rights reserved.

Scripture quotations taken from the Complete Jewish Bible (CJB). Copyright © 1998 by David H. Stern. All rights reserved. No portion of this book may be reproduced, stored in a retrieval system, or transmitted in any form or by any means without prior written permission of the publisher.

Scripture quotations taken from the Living Bible (TLB). Copyright © 1971 by Tyndale House Foundation. Used by permission of Tyndale House Publishers Inc., Carol Stream, Illinois 60188. All rights reserved.

Scripture quotations taken from the New King James Version (NKJV). Copyright © 1982 by Thomas Nelson, Inc. Used by permission. All rights reserved.

Paperback ISBN-13: 978-1-66288-863-2
Ebook ISBN-13: 978-1-66288-864-9

Table of Contents

About the Author vii
Acknowledgment ix
Psalm 77 1
About the Book: My Continuous Journey beyond
a Journey with God 3
A Journey and a Prayer 5
The Journey of Faith 7
A Journey beyond Belief 8
My Prayer for You 33
Personal Reflection: Your Faith Journey 35
Personal Obedience Prayer 36
End of Chapter Encouragement 37
A Journey with the Voice of God 39
The Voice of God 77
God Knows Your Name 78
Trusting God Today 79
Asking and Seeking 80
Believe or Doubt—You Choose 81
Prayer for Wisdom 82
My Prayer for You 83
Every Mountain High, Every Valley Low 84
A Prayer Inspired by Psalm 77 96
See Yourself in the Word of God 102
Moments along Your Journey 104

A Prayer of Inspiration from Psalm 27 108
Lift Up Your Head 111
He Has a Plan. 113
A Journey of Surrendering and Back
into the Father's Arms of Grace 114
Enough 129
Prayer: Prince of Peace. 130
A Journey beyond a Journey 131
A Continuous Journey. 136
Secret for The Journey 137

About the Author

Ayoka Brown is a daughter and friend to many. The name Ayoka means joy all around or someone who causes joy. She began her journey of faith at a very young age on the road less traveled, seeking to understand the knowledge of God's words and His presence daily. By doing so, she was able to build a stronger relationship with God and gain the deeper understanding of what it means to become a disciple for His Kingdom, by fighting and refusing to compromise her faith with the constant changes in society and culture.

Her desire in sharing this journey beyond a journey is to encourage anyone and everyone to seek a deeper relationship with our creator, the God of Abraham, Isaac, and Jacob—our Jehovah, our Elohim, and our Adonai; to understand that there are no limits or restrictions that could ever stop Him from loving you and wanting to walk side by side with you along life's journey. And know without a doubt that we all have full access to the throne room of His divine grace. If we are willing, then He is more than able to go above and beyond anything we could ever image or ask for.

I feel as though I have crossed many oceans, climbed many mountains, and sat in my fair share of valleys. And yet my walk seemed as though it was only just beginning. In the beginning of this journey I had a lot of excitement, as a child would when told they would be going to a theme park. But when the child realized that there were long lines before getting on their favorite ride, their excitement quickly melts away, as did my excitement when I realized there were things God had to strip away as I walk out this journey by surrendering all that I have been and all that I held on to, and by doing so, making room to identify His voice clearly during all the surrounding noise and distractions.

Surrendering my life and all that I held ever so dear to in the hands of God and picking up my cross just to follow where He leads has never been easy. And at times my fears whispered to me to turn back. However, I am thankful that God kept me and never let go of me through my many storms of questioning, fears, and doubts. But here I am to truly testify to the goodness of God.

God is always speaking; it is for us to be willing to listen and daring to follow through. Everything about this journey beyond a journey has to do with God and His directions.

To God Be the Glory.

Acknowledgment

Blessed are you, Lord our God, King of the universe, who gives wisdom generously and freely to all who ask without doubting. I am forever thankful to the Lord for the incredible people He has, by His grace, brought into my life. They have not only been my inspiration but my pillars and encouragers.

First, to my mom for your selfless love, strength, and prayers over me. To my dad, for being ever so present throughout this walk. Your presence has carried me more than you will ever know. And for this I am thankful for you always.

My big sister and big brother in Christ, for loving a perfectly imperfect stranger. Thank you for praying for me when at times I struggle to pray for myself. And thank you for being the godly pillars along this great journey of mountains and valleys.

To all my sisters in Christ at Restore Redeemed Contenders, I thank you all for your unconditional love, prayers, and encouragement. Though we all gathered through a crazy pandemic, God used that opportunity to create a sisterhood out of us.

A big thank you to those whom I have crossed paths with and have allowed themselves to be daring enough and believe in this book.

Finally, to you who have had to endure this journey with silence and patience. Greater things were yet to be done, and greater things have been done. I thank you for enduring this journey with me and thank you for praying.

Psalm 77

I cry aloud to God, aloud to God; and he hears me. On the day of my distress I am seeking Adonai; my hands are lifted up; my tears flow all night without ceasing; my heart refuses comfort. When remembering God, I moan; when I ponder, my spirit fails. You hold my eyelids and keep me from sleeping; I am too troubled to speak. I think about the days of old, the years of long ago; in the night I remember my song, I commune with myself, my spirit inquires: "Will Adonai reject forever? Will he never show his favor again? Has his grace permanently disappeared? Is his word to all generations done away? Has God forgotten to be compassionate? Has he in anger withheld his mercy?" Then I add, "That's my weakness—supposing the Most High's right hand could change." So I will remind myself of Yah's doings; yes, I will remember your wonders of old. I will meditate on your work and think about what you have done. God, your way is in holiness. What god is as great as God? You are the God who does wonders, you revealed your strength to the peoples. With your arm you redeemed your people, the descendants of Ya'akov and Yosef. The water saw you, God; the water saw you and writhed in anguish, agitated to its depths. The clouds poured water, the skies thundered, and your arrows flashed here and there. The sound of your thunder was in the whirlwind, the lightning flashes lit up the world, the earth trembled and shook. Your way went through the sea, your path through the turbulent waters; but your footsteps could not be traced. You led your people like a flock under the care of Moshe and Aharon.

—Psalm 77

About the Book:

My Continuous Journey Beyond a Journey with God

A journey beyond a journey is a lifelong relationship with God. It is not just about taking the road less traveled. It is about a pursuit of obedience to a God, who is the Father to the fatherless, a Friend to the friendless, a Comforter to the comfortless, and Savior risen King who is omnipresent. A God who seeks a heart that is willing to leave what is known by man's knowledge and walk the real journey of obedience and faith in this modern generation. A generation where compromising your faith and being forced to accept ungodly things is sadly the norm so that others can feel comfortable in their own sinful lust, and the lack of trust or reverence and belief in Adonai, a God who they have heard of and heard countless Bible stories of and a little bit of testimonies here and there. Yet they have never actually had an encounter with Him on a personal level. In the Word of God, it reminds us that "with a deep longing we will seek after God and require Him as a vital necessity. When we search for God with all our heart, we will find Him" (Jer. 29:13 AMP).

When we try to search for God in our ability and knowledge, it is like trying to find a needle in a haystack. But when we allow the Holy Spirit of God to dwell within us, direct us, and lead us in every aspect of our lives, oh, the wonders and mysteries of treasures in God we find. That journey with the Spirit of God guiding us, not even we could ever fathom how we got over those mountains and walk those thousands of miles through the many storms of life.

Nobody knows the blueprint of this journey but God. The mission of faith and full obedience to God is never for the swift, and the battles that rise along the way for the strong. Neither is it for the wisest of men nor favored by men of ability (Eccles. 9:11).

However, it is for a heart that is willing to be broken by God and to be used by Him. There is a saying that goes like this: "The wisdom of man is the foolishness of God, and the wisdom of God is the foolishness of man." Remember, God did not call the qualified. Those whom He called, He qualified them and equipped them with tools to accomplish the work.

Never in my wildest dream had I ever seen myself becoming an author and writing books. I certainly did not see myself as qualified enough to write a book or as having the full experience and knowledge. However, when God has an appointed time for you, you might feel or think that you are not qualified. Please remember this: God already qualified you. He called you out of the hiding place or instead the holding position, which has been a training ground and growth for you. I indeed can testify to this in every way.

For some unforeseen reason, God gave me this scripture when He called me to begin this journey of faith and obedience. It has carried me through every season.

Hebrews 11:8–9: "By faith, Abraham obeyed when he was called, to go out to the place which he would receive as an inheritance. And he went out, not knowing where he was going. By faith he dwelt in the land of promise as in a foreign country, dwelling in tents with Isaac and Jacob, the heirs with him of the same promise."

Remember, the calling and blessing on your life is not just for you. This blessing goes beyond you and your generation. It is food for the hungry; it is life for lifeless, hope for the hopeless, and a compass for those who are lost and broken. Your journey of faith and obedience in the will of God is a beacon of light paving the way back to the Father's heart for those not knowing the way.

A Journey and a Prayer

Shine Your light through this broken vessel
Let them see Your unconditional love pouring through this vessel
Let them know Your Mercy and Grace through these broken pieces
Teach them Your ways through this healed vessel
Give this vessel Your Grace to remain standing and
Your strength to keep enduring this journey
Let Your presence always and forever be with this vessel
My life is forever on You, my solid rock and foundation
You are my hiding place, my strong tower, my safe refuge
You are my light guiding me through many seas
You are my ship sailing strong through life's journey
Let Your Name be glorified, O Lord, through my heart to the heavens
Let Your Love in this vessel continue to be the anchor which
Keeps my soul and spirit grounded in You, Lord
Let all the days fashioned for this vessel be fulfilled, O God, in You
With purpose and passion giving You glory
Every step of the way
Let my obedience continuously be pleasing to
Your heart and in Your sight
As Your every Word continues to be my stepping
Stone and cornerstone
Let this journey beyond a journey forever be
My walk with You every step of the way

A Journey Beyond A Journey

Through the rain, through the thunder, through the lightning
Through the hail, through the snow
Through the twisters, through the tornados
Through the rising of the sun and until
The going down of the same
Lord, You are my journey beyond a journey

The Journey of Faith

※※

By faith, Abraham obeyed when he was called to go out to the place which he would receive as an inheritance. And he went out, not knowing where he was going. By faith, he dwelt in the land of promise as in a foreign country, living in tents with Isaac and Jacob, the heirs with him of the same promise. For he waited for the city which has foundations, whose builder and maker is God.

Hebrews 11:8–10

A Journey Beyond Belief

There is a level of faith that we are all given. God gave us all a measure of faith, and how we choose to use it or where we place it is our decision. This kind of faith can be best known as "the mustard seed faith."

Luke 17:6 (AMP) says:

> And the Lord said, "If you have confident, abiding faith in God even as small as a mustard seed, you could say to this mulberry tree which has strong roots, 'be pulled up by the roots and be planted in the sea," and if the request were in agreement with the will of God, it would have obeyed you.

A mustard seed is only two millimeters and can grow six to 20 feet high and spread 20 feet across with its branches. Its roots run deep into the soil and keep the land around it healthy. It can also deal with poor soil and extreme heat.

Can you imagine your faith rooted so deeply in the very heart and Word of God and spread so vastly across the hearts of believers and unbelievers lives? Such strength—such a boost in their faith along their journey.

Mark 4:31–32 (NKJV) says:

> It is like a mustard seed which, when established on the ground, is smaller than all the seeds on earth. And when sown, it grows up and becomes greater than all herbs, and shoots out large branches. So that the birds of the air may nest under its shade.

This is in reflection to Psalm 91:1–2:

In our everyday walk in our countries, cities, local communities, and our neighborhoods, our faith and trust come under pressure—our ways of life, our walk with our neighbors, our friends, and family.

As crazy and busy as our surroundings are, our faith withstands more than what we can ever imagine in one moment. Now just as the mustard seed can grow six to 20 feet high and its branches spread 20 feet across, our faith can rise above and beyond such heights and develop deeper roots. Faith gives us the confidence and opportunity with the grace of God to boldly have a relationship with Him. His mercy is everlasting and unconditional. We have the freedom to believe in Him and trust Him and walk in obedience with His will, plan, and purpose for our lives, also, understanding that no matter what we have done in the past, present, or future, He is faithful and will forever be at our side.

One of the greatest things about faith is that for some unforeseen reason you know where it is coming from, but you cannot see the full path it is taking you. This kind of faith requires one more thing: trust. Trusting in God no matter how the journey may feel or seem to be a never-ending battle and cycle. That is why I believe the apostle Paul tells us in Hebrews 11:1–2 (NCV):

> "Faith means being sure of the things we hope for and knowing that something is real even if we do not see it."

There are many times I have fought and, well, still occasionally fight, not to overlook this verse and come to a deeper understanding of it during my most frustrating moments. I have seen countless times where my frustration has caused me to either second-guess, question, or doubt many things God would or has shared with me. In my moment of frustration, I placed a limit on what was shared and trusted with me. I found myself putting a time frame on things I prayed for and many other blessings God revealed to me, which were to come to pass. However, God never gave me a specific time of when and how I was to receive what I asked for in prayer.

We must be very careful not to allow ourselves to get so caught up putting a limit or time frame on God, His promises, His Word, or His abilities to meet our every need, great or small. I believe this is where many of us get stuck. We get stuck on the time frame created in our minds because we are in such a rush. Here is how we want our blessing, and this is how long we are willing to give you, God, to make it happen. The sad part about all of that is, none of that is showing real faith and trust in God. It shows how very little we know of God and the lack of relationship with Him.

God is not a genie in a lamp. Where your faith in rubbing the lamp for Him to appear and grant you three wishes immediately. Now, if this were the case, then we would all be doomed from start to finish. All of us would have a lamp wishing for the good, the bad, and the ugly toward each other. I, for one, am thankful that God is not a genie in a bottle to rub and grant me three wishes. God alone knows what is best for us, better than we do. He knows that our needs are more significant than our wants. And what we want is not necessarily what we need to help us grow into the man or woman He created us to be.

The genie only gives you what you want, but God gives you what you need. See Psalm 37:4.

So many times we find ourselves wanting to take a sneak peek at the promised blessing before believing it. And even at times when we see it, we struggle to comprehend the reality of how possible the impossible is with God. Somehow, we try to find fault with the blessing after it comes, questioning the way it looks or the way it sounds, maybe the size of it, the color, and whether we are good enough for it or we are worthy of such a blessing.

We need to stop trying to talk ourselves out of our own blessings, which we have prayed for.

How does this sound to you? Better yet, how do you think it looks and sounds like to God? I believe this makes us look ungrateful to God. Who is always going above and beyond to exceed what we dare to ask Him for? We need to recognize how great His love is for us, that He would move Heaven on earth for us. To me, this makes our faith in God seem as though it is all over the place and not stable in Him. It is as though we know that God gives good gifts and have seen the evidence of it. So rather than developing a deeper relationship with Him, we just want to take His gifts and any other blessings we can get our hands on and dash through the doors. The only time we return to Him is when we are low on a miracle. Today this would be considered as abuse. Abuse on our father's loving kindness towards us and taking advantage of his mercy.

Is our Heavenly Father not much more than this? Does He not deserve a better honor than that? Today, take a moment and ask yourself, "How do I see God? How can I honor Him with my obedience? How can I invest at least some of my time to develop a deep and meaningful relationship with God?"

Having our faith grounded in God is like an anchor on a ship. When that ship drops its anchor to hold it in place, it does not matter how rough the sea and its waves are. That anchor is going to hold its ground and keep that ship in place. Essentially this is the same with our faith in God, our walk with Him, and our trust in Him.

If we have faith in God, then we trust Him; if we believe in God, then we have faith in Him. Nothing more and nothing less, there should not be any room to question or doubt it.

Have you ever stopped to think about what faith is and what it means to you? Ask yourself, what does faith look like to me? And where have I placed my hope? I ask a few of my close friends in Christ, whom I have met along my journey of faith. They are born-again Christians and were raised in different cultures and countries. I selected the following responses to what faith is and means to them:

> "Faith is the ability to believe in things that are impossible or unbelievable. Believe when there is no hope, believe when the situation prevents you from having a light of hope. Faith means to be bold, courageous, crazy sometimes, and requires perseverance."

> "Faith looks like the flame of a candle in the darkness. It is that little light that tries to shine through the dark. This little light that you want to follow when there is nowhere else to go. You want to hold on to it because there is no other way through that situation."

> "To me, faith is trusting God with things He has spoken or that He has manifested to me. Faith is trusting God with everything in my life. My interpretation of faith is the manifestation of things coming to the present. These are the Word of God that has been spoken and coming to life. Faith, for me, looks like two large hands with a beautiful light behind it, because it is God's hands. That is how I can picture Faith because God is the giver of all things that are in His will."

> "Faith, to me, is a choice. It believes in something without having the proof first. I know that faith has different meanings for different people. And some people have faith in other people, but for me, it is more spiritual.

For me, faith means recognizing that the world does not revolve around me. That there are factors in my life which I will never have control over. I have faith in God (Heavenly Father) to watch over myself, my family, to protect me, and for guidance."

"I do not think faith looks like anything because it is believing in the unseen and is internal. However, if I look at a person (not judging), I would be able to determine if their faith was birthed on something due to their actions. In my understanding, it can be anything. So long as it shows a subject making irrational decisions. And decisions are all based on his/her faith.

For example, if you witnessed me walking at night down a street in the pitch-black. There is no form of light to guide my steps. To you, I may need a flashlight to help me see. And the further I go, the darker it became to your visible eyes. However, for me, I can see perfectly fine. My Faith in God is my light, trusting His guidance for my path. I have the faith to believe and the courage to trust Him. There is a saying, 'We walk by faith, not by sight.'"

"Faith is the belief in the things we hope. Faith is believing in something that may not make sense at this moment. In my life, it believes God can do what looks impossible to me. For example, I don't know how we are going to afford my son's school, but I am believing."

"What does faith look like to me? To be honest, it has been something I have been struggling with the past few years. It is because of my family, and its living situation.

However, I have decided that contemplating what happened will not solve anything. I am putting my trust in God, being positive, reading, and listening to the Word more about faith. Also reminding myself that I had no idea how I was going to move to America. At the time, every step and decision to marry Patrick was by Faith and Faith only. So, I am deciding to go back to that mindset."

"Faith is trusting God for my present and my future. Knowing that what He did in the past or other people's life, He can do it again. In my experience, it means to keep on going even if I don't understand His ways. Keep on having hope in what He told personally, even when time passes by and I do not see anything happening right now. Sometimes God shows me something, and I find it hard to believe it at that moment. Then out of nowhere, it happens before my eyes. And He's [God] like, "I told you." I regret it so much because He's trustworthy. For all those times, I did not trust Him, and I want to trust Him fully now!"

"Faith is like a natural breath. Every day you wake up knowing that everything is going to be okay, and God is in control. For me, faith cannot be explained because it is experienced daily. You decide to believe despite the circumstance. In my life, confidence grows with what God does—what He says to me and I can see these things come to reality. To me, faith is a lot of things and events revealed in intimate moments with trusting God. Faith was part of a decision to believe. It was nourished by the revealed Word of God and the exhaled prayers."

A Journey Beyond Belief

For those who do not believe that they have faith, I just want to make you aware that everyone exercises faith daily. For instance, when you go to sit in a chair, do you inspect it thoroughly before you sit in it? Of course not. You just trust that it will hold you as you sit in it. That is called faith. The problem is that we choose to put our faith in all the wrong things when it comes to believing and trusting God..

Everyone was blessed with a measure of faith, whether we choose to accept it. Now, what we decide to do with it and place it in is our choice. Faith is and will always be a part of our lives, and the journey endures. It is in our DNA, no matter the color of our skin, the way we dress, the language we speak, or what country we live in, great or small.

I have come to realize that faith is the essence of my walk and my relationship with God. I had to reach a place where choosing to accept that what is impossible to man is possible with God. I had to start believing, even though what I had thought of was not in sight.

Every time I hear anyone begin to talk about faith, the only name which continuously comes to my heart is Abraham. Hebrews 11, verses 8 to 9, says, "It was by faith that Abraham obeyed when God called him to leave home and go to another land that God would give him as an inheritance. He went without knowing where he was going. And even when he reached the land God promised him, he lived there by faith, for he was like a foreigner, living in tents."

I never understood why God persistently gave me this scripture as I began writing in obedience. It is only now that I have a deeper understanding as to why and how it pertains to my journey with Him.

My mustard seed faith began to grow the moment I started asking questions about God, seeking to know more about who God was, His voice, what I mean to Him, and finding His secret hiding place.

My faith growing up was as easy as one, two, three. Growing up and watching my grandma live and walk a life of faith was inspiring: the way she would sit in His presence under the mango tree; the way she would encourage me about who God was, how great He is, and how powerful He is. Through her walk, her worship and love for God,

I found myself falling in love with God and wanted to get to know Him as my grandma did.

Hearing God's voice then was a constant guide to my every step because I believed without a doubt. My physical sight was not fully formed much as my spiritual sight. So, it is safe to say God used that moment to strengthen my confidence in Him and with everything around. Through my spiritual views as a child, God walked me along my young journey. He was showing me how to have faith honestly; not just in Him, but also in the things He would speak to me about and show me in advance. These things would then manifest right before my very eyes, leaving me in awe. For example, witnessing a child who had just seen a magic trick and was speechless. However, this was no trick or more, so it was real life. His glory was being shown to me little by little.

Many people would call me strange because they were not able to fully understand the depth of my walk with God and have not been able to witness many of the things shown to me through the Holy Spirit. As a child and spoken to about matters beyond one's understanding, comprehension and the greatness of God and His infinite wisdom. People thought that I was crazy when I would go up to them to deliver a message from the Holy Spirit. To see a little child come up to you, revealing things that only you and God should know, would be somewhat worrying.

However, little did they know that, I thought that I was going crazy. Especially when they denied the word spoken through me to them, sometimes I would ask God, "Hey, did You get it wrong?" Think about it, when has God ever gotten it wrong? Never!

How many of us think that we are or made to believe that we are crazy because we hear from God? Have you ever looked up the meaning of the word "crazy"? The term "crazy" means not mentally sound, insane, marked by thought or action that lacks reason, impractical, being out of the ordinary and unusual.

Now, would you classify yourself in any of these regarding being called crazy because you hear from God?

When we walk with God, listen to Him and follow His direction; most of the things He asks us to do will sound crazy. I think it is because we believe in a God whom we have never seen. And for somebody who never believed as we do, all of this would sound crazy. They will never be able to fathom such faith without a relationship of their own with and in God.

There was a man who never saw the rain before. He was a just man and was perfect in his generations. God gave him instructions to build a boat with specific dimensions. This man was Noah, who had never done something like this, much less seen it before. Noah received further guidance regarding who and what should be in it. Talk about crazy faith! Can you imagine refined faith in God? Who in their right mind would be building an extremely large boat in a drought? Well, not just a drought but in a time where they had never ever had rain before.

This, to me and maybe you, can be perceived as unspeakable, incomprehensible faith.

God wants our mind out of the way so that we can be led by the Holy Spirit. We are not mind led, but we are Spirit led to go above and beyond the natural man and the mind of impossibilities that are unseen, whereby we do not have to rely on seeing it and touching it to believe but rather believe without touching or seeing it first.

Let's look at it this way: have you ever seen tomorrow before? We go throughout today and all the duties we all carry out. Then night falls, and we prepare ourselves for bed and hope or rather have faith that when we wake up it will be tomorrow. Can you see how there is faith there? However, somehow, we have not considered this as faith—faith in knowing that with the grace of God, we will enter tomorrow where many others have not.

How many of your friends would believe in you and support you if you were to share with them something sounding as crazy as what God asked Noah to do? How would they look at you? Would they truly comprehend the words coming from your mouth? What would they reply to you upon hearing such instructions? Would this deter you from being obedient to what God has called you to do based on their opinion and lack of understanding of God's direct instructions to you?

Sadly, many of us get deterred from following God because we value our families' and friends' opinions higher than God, who, by the way, is the one calling us to repentance and into His divine light. Too many of us hold the opinion of man higher than God. We forget that those same ones God Himself created too, and has a path for them, a calling and a season of growth and blessing with their own name on it.

Now they may never share with you what God has revealed to them in secret but require you to share what He is leading you to.

Please ask yourself this question: why would God ask or need their permission to take you out of your bondage and lead you into a blessing that is running over, because you chose to pick up your own cross to follow Him? We must be extremely careful what we share pertaining to our calling because it isn't everyone in that season who God will allow to tag along, if any. Sometimes He will shake the branches just so that you can be free from the heaviness of negative individuals and to open your eyes to see the hindrances before you.

When we move in faith, and through faith it makes no sense to logical thinking.

When it comes to our spiritual wellbeing, we need to be in obedience to God and not man. He knows the thoughts He thinks toward us. These are thoughts of peace and not of evil. It is to give us a better future and hope we have never experienced before.

I am pretty sure that the people surrounding Noah thought he lost all his marbles. They had never seen anything like it, much less had they believed an inviable God, as he did. God was going to flood the entire earth, which was unimaginable because they had never seen rain before in their lives. However, this did not stop Noah because he believed in God. Sure, he may have had questions just like you and I would, but still God trusted Noah, proved to him and provided the means for him to follow through with his instructions.

It was indeed crazy when Noah was building the Ark, but it was faith when it began to rain. Noah did not have to see the flood to believe it was about to flood, because he believed in the one who told him and instructed him to. How many of us can truly say that when God knocks on the windows of our hearts and asks us to do something that our flesh would not scream out, making all different type of excuses as to why not to be obedient? Would we still put our flesh under submission of the Spirit of God, willing, trusting His direction and do it anyway?

I have been on this journey long enough to learn that not everyone will believe in the calling on your life, nor will they comprehend it. And you know what? That is perfectly okay. Who is to say that God even wants them to see what He is doing in your life in that season? Who said that they needed to? Does God have to ask their permission to use you in His divine will? We each have our path with our measure of faith from God. How we choose to be obedient falls on us. What excuse will you give to God for not being obedient to his instructions in your life? I don't think you can blame someone else.

How many of us have ever watched a seed grow up from the earth and sprout up? Personally, I have not, but somehow, I can only imagine planting a bell pepper seed in a flowerpot, covering it with the soil not too deep because I still want it to have a little room to sprout up freely and not just drown deep in the soil and not grow. I do not have to see how it sprouts up; however, I must make sure that it is rooted in the right soil, watered and exposing it to sunlight and then leave the rest to God.

> "I planted, Apollos watered, but God was causing the growth. So then neither the one who plants nor the one who waters is anything, but God who causes the growth. Now the one who plants and the one who waters are one; but each will receive his own reward according to his own labor" (1 Cor. 3:6–8).

Where are we planting our seed of faith in, or rather, who are we planting it in? As much as we are instructed to renew our minds daily, I also believe we ought to check our daily soil and the seeds we are planting. Whose soil is this, who sent it, where did it come from, is this the right soil to plant my seed in, and most of all, are we asking God, "Is this deeply rooted in Your Kingdom?"

> "The Sower went out to sow his seed; and as he sowed, some fell beside the road, and it was trampled underfoot, and the birds of the sky ate it up. Other seed fell on rocky soil, and when it came up, it withered away because it had no moisture. Other seed fell among the thorns; and the thorns grew up with it and choked it out. And yet other seed fell into the good soil, and grew up, and produced a crop a hundred times as much." As He said these things, He would call out, 'The one who has ears to hear, let him hear'" (Luke 8:5–8).

"Now this is the parable: the seed is the word of God. And those beside the road are the ones who have heard, then the devil comes and takes away the word from their heart, so that they will not believe and be saved. Those on the rocky soil are the ones who, when they hear, receive the word with joy; and yet these do not have a firm root; they believe for a while, and in a time of temptation they fall away. And the seed which fell among the thorns, these are the ones who have heard, and as they go on their way they are choked by worries, riches, and pleasures of this life, and they bring no fruit to maturity. But the seed in the good soil, these are the ones who have heard the word with a good and virtuous heart, and hold it firmly, and produce fruit with perseverance" (Luke 11–15).

Yes, it may be discouraging at times when those who surround you do not believe. However, you must remember who called you in the first place. Who equipped you and who gave you the instruction? Jesus is the author and finisher of our faith. No matter how great the task given to us is, God will and has already provided everything for us to accomplish it.

Always remember, everything that seems crazy in His divine will He has ordained it to happen. Not everybody will agree, and they will not be able to clap for your breakthrough or rejoice with you. And when you get a vision from God, that is you hearing from God, please live your life based on your faith in Him and His trust in you to accomplish all He has directed you to. Other people's faith and trust in Him can only take you so far but not the full journey that He has paved out for you. So, step out of your comfort zone and disregard the opinion of others.

Think about the woman with the issues of blood for 12 years in the Bible. In her time, it was not permitted for her to be out among the public because she was considered unclean. Furthermore, anyone she touched would be considered unclean until evening and they would have to wash themselves in the sea. And anything she touched or sat on would be unclean. So, in all, she would have had to isolate herself. This would mean not being able to go to the marketplace or go into the temple of God to worship and to ever leave an offering. Can you imagine the strain it put on her confidence and even to believe that she is someone worthy of anything or received love from her family, community leaders? She tried everything that money could buy, and it was all a dead end. I could only imagine that her hope was low, and she had nothing left to hope for. She must have felt depressed and lonely, until she heard about Yeshua, who had been doing miracles, signs, and wonders, and His teachings gave her hope to believe and stirred up a fire in her to hope like never before, and she believed without a doubt.

She was already cast out by society, deemed unhealthy and unclean. So, she really did not have anything to lose by daring to step out in faith to reach Him by any means necessary. It had been 12 years since this hemorrhage began, and there had been no sign of relief until now upon hearing about Yeshua.

Can you imagine the courage it took her to step out? But the only thing she could focus on was getting to Yeshua by any means. Even if she couldn't speak with Him, touching the hem of His garment was enough for her. Only faith in the unseen could have moved her. She could not see her healing, however, she believed for it. She was hungry for it and knew how precious it was to receive her life and freedom back from this bondage.

Let me ask you, what have you been longing for God to break, heal and set you free from? Have you asked while believing or have you been asking without believing? Can you believe to get on a bus without standing at the bus stop for it?

> "What good is it, my brother, if someone claims to have faith but has no action to prove it? Is such "faith" able to save him? Suppose a brother or sister is without clothes and daily food, and someone says to him, "shalom! Keep warm and eat healthy!" without giving him what he needs, what good does it do? Thus, faith by itself, unaccompanied by action, is dead. But someone will say that you have faith and I have actions. Show me this faith of yours without actions, and I will show you my faith by my actions! You believe that God is One good for you! The demons believe too-the thought makes them shudder with fear!" (James 2:14-19)

Many of us are still stuck and have become so complacent in our infirmities that we no longer seek to reach out and touch and call upon the Lord for our healing. We have become too comfortable within this comfort zone, believing that we can develop and grow there, but little do we know that this is not the case. Just as how we place a mustard seed in a tiny pot, knowing its full potential to grow, we, however, refuse to repot it into deeper soil in an open space for it to grow to its true potential. The seed will never grow to its true potential if placed in a tiny pot, just like us. If we sit in our comfort zone and expect an abundance of overflow, there would not be any room to contain any of it.

This woman believed by hearing about what He had been going around doing. How many times has God revealed to us, and yet we fail to believe Him? How long must we sit in our everyday infirmities and not want to be free from it all, when there is a Savior waiting for us to surrender all to Him and allow His presence to change us? When will we be sick and tired of making a mess of things and doing it over and over our way, which forever leads us to a dead end?

This woman had one goal, and that was to reach Jesus and to receive her healing, no matter what the crowd or the leaders of the synagogue would say. She was not going to allow this opportunity to pass her by. So, my question is, why have we allowed so many godly opportunities pass us out of fear of man's opinion? Is their opinion higher than the Most High God? Did they carry the cross for you? Were they the ones who gave their life for you up on the cross at Calvary?

No one knows you better than God does, no one knows your heart like God, and no one can heal you like He can. So, trust in Him and have faith in Him alone. He will guide you through. No matter the depth of the valley or the heights of the mountains you are facing today. He will and He can, just believe.

> "And suddenly, a woman who had a flow of blood for twelve years came from behind and touched the hem of His garment. For she said to herself, "If only I may touch His garment, I shall be made well." But Jesus turned around, and when He saw her, He said, "Be of good cheer, daughter; your faith has made you well." And the woman was made well from that hour" (Matt. 9:20–22).

Her action had to align up with her faith and her faith had to align up with her action.

If she can believe in Him for her healing, so can we. The same God then is also the same God now. She did not have to pay Him with silver or gold nor sell her soul to the devil. She simply believed not that He could but that He would. It was her faith in Him. This is the place that we all need to reach, walking along our journey with Him. And this is the decision we all need to make today because many of us has started this journey but somehow along the way got scared, sidetracked, distracted by the enticement of what society is offering get rich quick scheme, buying the most expensive products because it heals you better. By placing our faith and trust in these things has redirected us from our first love who is God.

When was God never enough for us? Or anything He perfected was not perfect and fulfilling?

Our faith in Him sets us free from the chains of destruction over our lives and our family's lives. And we must be willing to do it His way because our ways are destructive. We were never created to live without Him or go through this life without Him.

> "But You, Lord, are a shield around me, My glory, and the One who lifts my head" (Ps. 3:3).

There is no doubt that you wouldn't see the manifestation of God in your life because of your faith. Nobody thought that Noah had any sense until it began raining, and the wildest of animals walked onto the Ark without attacking each other.

What might seem crazy in one season will always be counted in another. The crazy season is preparing you for that mountaintop view. Being in the valley appears absurd, but reaching the mountaintop is the evidence of the journey and the victory.

Noah's obedience was the perfect example of this.

There have been many moments on my journey when God gave and instructed me to do or deliver messages to people. As confident as I was at the time, I was still a big chicken. Oh, yes, I sure was. Now, was it because I feared to talk, or was it because I feared what people might think of me? Well, it was a little of both. To know someone and to know their walk with God are two very different things.

I was still in my mid-teens when God gave me a message to deliver to a lady. At first, I was taken back by the message because it felt too real. Was it a dream, or was it a vision, I kept asking myself over and over. The information was playing over and over in my spirit with the voice of God. And no matter what I did that day, the Holy Spirit kept repeating, "You need to deliver the message."

Now, let me say this, whenever you receive a specific message from God to deliver, please do not keep it to yourself. The information does not belong to you. It is for the person God decided, and it is their evidence that God sees and knows their situation and also to give them hope to hold on because God is busy working on their behalf.

How would you feel if someone held onto your life-changing message that could save you from destruction or bless everything about your life?

In the same way, it is like the mailman who delivers the mail in your area. It is against the law for him to steal your mail and keep it for himself. The same applies to a spiritual message from God. To that person, it may be a life-and-death situation for deliverance.

Now at first, I did not deliver the message straight away. I brought it to my mother's attention. My mother immediately stopped me before I could finish explaining what God had given me to share. She said to me, "Ayoka, there is a reason why God has entrusted you with this message. This message is not for me to hear. This message is for the person who He told you to deliver it. You do not have to understand the message because it is not for you. And whatever you do not understand, go back to God, and ask Him for clarity. The only way you will have peace and be able to rest is if you obey and deliver that message."

After hearing what my mother had to say, I followed through with what she advised me to do. I only did maybe five percent of delivering the message with a question. That was only to see if God was on point with the information, He gave me to present.

Was I wrong in questioning God? Yes and no! God knew that I would because His message never changed. His answer to me three nights in a row was the same, and His instructions remained the same. And all He needed was my obedience, my trust, and faith in Him.

Eventually, before the week was up, I could no longer question God and what was asked of me to deliver. My heart and spirit could not rest until I sat with the lady and gave her the message. My fear told me, "She will never accept the message and think that you are crazy," while my spirit convicted me for holding onto a message I knew, without a doubt, God had entrusted me to deliver.

The fact is we will never know or see the prayers a person has been praying for their breakthrough. And if you are already in position with where God has you, He will use you to fulfill the needs or confirm His promises for any of your brothers and sisters. All that will ever be required of you is a willing heart that seeks to be used by Him, to trust Him and have faith in the unseen.

Now, why would God have revealed to me that this lady was pregnant before she knew? Out of the entire message, I felt as though God knew this would cause me to question. I asked the lady on two separate occasions, just to try and see whether what God told me was true. She thought my question was very odd but could not comprehend.

You and I both know that this was and is not what faith is. Instead, I was trying to see the word spoken instead of believing the word spoken. And the Bible teaches us that faith is the substance of things hoped for and the evidence of things we cannot see. I asked the question, not because I doubted God but because I was trying to see to believe instead of fully trusting and just merely obeying.

Faith is simple if you just believe, instead of delaying and waiting to see it before you think about it. That is not how faith works. It never has, and it never will.

Not only was I given a message to deliver, but I also was shown the unborn child and its sex. God always has His divine reasons behind everything He says and does. You and I do not have to understand it or see the full results of it. However, we do need to remain obedient as we walk hand in hand with Him, trusting Him wholeheartedly in every aspect of our journey in faith.

Eventually, that week, the lady, and I met up. I explained to her why I was asking the questions and delivered the full message from God. To my astonishment, she broke down and began to cry. She was explaining and confirming that she had not been making time for God but would try. As for the other matter of pregnancy, she still did not know if she was but would trust God in that matter.

Look at how God is about to prove His word by getting all the glory while building my faith and trust in Him. About two weeks after meeting up with that lady, I went on a vacation to one of the Caribbean islands. During the second week, my spirit led me to extend it for another week. And just as I followed through with extending my vacation, I received a message from the lady telling me that she and her husband were in the hospital. They found out that she was pregnant, but she had not been feeling well. So, they went to the emergency room, where she had a miscarriage.

They revealed to me that their baby was indeed a little boy and told me his name. Once I heard the name, that was it for me because God had showed me the name of their son. I was astounded; my mind was in awe of God. Everything in the message I delivered had come to the present fully, as God said. God causes all things to work together for our good and His glory, to show who He is and how great He is.

This situation could have caused this young couple to turn away from God. However, instead, they held on to each other and held on to the unconditional love of God. They were trusting and believing that

He can and will restore what was lost. God did indeed prove it to them and restored everything and more as they sought Him.

One of the many things I took away from this was that no matter what, God never gets it wrong. God says what He means, and He means what He says. His word does not fall to the ground, nor does it ever return to Him void, even if we chose to take Him at His word.

God revealed to me the things that were to be, but they were not yet revealed. Wow!

> Awake, awake, put on strength, O arm of the Lord;
> Awake as in the days of old, the generations of long ago.
> Was it not You who cut Rahab in pieces, who pierced the dragon?
>
> Was it not You who dried up the sea, the waters of the great deep; who made the depths of the sea a pathway for the redeemed to cross over? And the redeemed of the Lord will return
>
> And come to Zion with joyful shouting, and everlasting joy will be on their heads.
>
> They will obtain gladness and joy, and sorrow and sighing will flee away.
>
> —Isaiah 51:9–11

The mysteries of God are spiritual truths that are known by revelations. God reveals His mysteries to those who are available, obedient to the gospel, and who are seeking the mysteries of His Kingdom. As the word of God says in the book of Jeremiah 55:8–11:

> For My thoughts are not your thoughts, nor are your ways My ways," declares the Lord. "For as the heavens are higher than the earth, so are My ways higher than your ways and My thoughts than your thoughts. For as the rain and the snow come down from heaven, And do not return there without watering the earth And making it produce and sprout, And providing seed to the Sower and bread to the eater; So will My word be which goes out of My mouth; It will not return to Me empty, without accomplishing what I desire, and without succeeding in the purpose for which I sent it.

Can you imagine how many times have we fell short of His glory? How many times have we had to seek His presence for something we have disobeyed Him on, and yet, still His divine mercy, love, and grace never fails to meet us where we are, giving us another opportunity to try again, to breathe again, to seek Him, and to discipline ourselves enough to spend time in His presence. Heavenly Father, may You forgive us for the many times we fail and have fallen short by being disobedient, getting in Your way and blocking our own blessings, not just for ourselves but for those around us and their breakthroughs.

Now you might be asking, which I also asked, what is the Gospel of God's Kingdom? And the answer I got from the Holy Spirit was this: "The Gospel of the Kingdom of God is the good news and understanding that there is only one way into the Kingdom. His name is Yeshua (God saves), and He is fully God and fully man. He came to earth specifically to die for the world to bring atonement as the ultimate and only possible sacrifice for our sins by living a sinless life, always doing His Abba's will. He died and resurrected so that we can now call Him Abba (Father) our Abba and live eternally in the Kingdom of Heaven with Him upon our death on earth."

The Gospel is the Good News, and the Good News is the Gospel. It is the news of who Jesus is, what He has done, and how all that He did changes everything for you and me.

For you and I this means that we can now eternally be close to God, the God of Isaac, Jacob, and Abraham, who is the creator of the Heavens and Earth, the Alpha and Omega, our Elohim, our El Shaddi, our Adonai.

Imagine we are no longer required to build an altar and bring a lamb to sacrifice as a burnt offering. Or even give our sacrifices to a priest at the temple once a year to atone for our sins. They alone could enter the tabernacle and the Holy of Holies because of what Jesus (Yeshua) did for us all and was our ultimate sacrifice atonement for our sin. By laying down His life for you and me, we no longer need to go through all of that anymore.

Psalm 51:17 reminds us of this: "You do not take pleasure in burnt offering. The sacrifices of God are a broken spirit; A broken and a contrite heart, God, you will not despise."

Our Heavenly Father just wants our rendered heart and not clothing inward nor outward expression of love and obedience.

We must remember that God has always been there since the beginning. All things came to be through Him. And without Him, nothing made had being. But to as many as did receive Him to those who put their trust in His person and power. He gave the right to become children of God and not because of bloodline but because of God.

My friends, the Word became a human being and lived with us. We saw the "Shekinah." The "Shekinah" of the Father's Son, full of grace and truth. Yes, it is true that no one has ever seen God but the only unique Son, who is identical with God and is at the Father' side. Jesus (Yeshua) has made Him known. He came as a light in the darkness to show us the way to become children of God, as the Kingdom of God in the Kingdom of Heaven.

"In the beginning was the Word, and the Word was with God, and the Word was God" (John 1:1).

"In the beginning God created the heavens and the earth" (Gen. 1:1).

"Then God said, 'Let there be light'; and there was light" (Gen. 1:3).

"In him was life, and the life was the light of mankind" (John 1:4).

"God saw that the light was good, and God divided the light from the darkness" (Gen. 1:4).

As I often asked myself this question, I would like to ask you also. Are you ready for the Kingdom of God to come, if He was to knock on your front door, the windows of your heart, your car door, your doorsteps, your job, interrupt the middle of your favorite movie, watching your favorite sports team, your dance routine, or even you listening to your favorite pastor preaching the house down?

Could you truly say that you are ready? Or that you are willing to give it all up to follow and do His will no matter where He may lead you? I believe this is something we all need to ask ourselves by seeking the face of God and sit awhile in His Presence to know who it is we are living for and serving.

God is available and willing. The real question that we need to ask ourselves is, are we ready to lay all of who we are and have become, to behold the beauty of His righteousness, His holiness to be renewed and change, allowing His light, love, and grace to shine in and through us?

My friend, nothing misses the Father, and nothing can be done without His presence. With Him nothing can ever be impossible, but without Him you will only be dragging your tail day in and day out in this life without knowing Him. You will only keep hitting the dead-end signs.

However, you will have everything to gain with Him in your life and on your side.

My Prayer for You

Heavenly Father, the creator of the Heavens and of the Earth. Our Elohim, we pray that you open the eyes of our hearts so that we can receive You fully and be changed by Your divine touch. May Your presence in our lives cause us to fall at Your feet, humbling ourselves, surrendering who we are and who we have allowed ourselves to become, and allow You to restore us into the light and love who You have created us to be. We know that we have fallen short of Your glory, but, because of Your Son giving His life for us, we are renewed in the light of Your glory. So, we come before You and ask for a fresh anointing. Break our hearts with all that breaks Yours, renew Your spirit within us as we seek Your face. Help us to renew our minds daily with Your Word and lead us with Your Holy Spirit. We have tried many things on our own and have been on many journeys that we believe we could have handled on our own. However, every path we chose without You has been a dead end. So, this time we desire to walk this new journey with you teaching and guiding us for Your glory. Father, as You continue to watch over us, may Your Presence be a constant reminder for us to surrender to You, Your will, and most of all put You first in all that we do. We pray this in the precious and holy name of Yeshua (Jesus). Amen.

"Even now," says the Lord, "Turn and come to Me with all your heart in genuine repentance, with fasting and weeping and mourning until every barrier is removed and the broken fellowship is restored; Rip your heart to pieces in sorrow and contrition and not your garments." Now return in repentance to the Lord your God, For He is gracious and compassionate, Slow to anger, abounding in lovingkindness faithful to His covenant with His people.

—Joel 2:12–13

Personal Reflection: Your Faith Journey

Personal reflection on your journey of faith: What is your faith journey like right now?

Take a few moments to recap and write about that one time God took your faith to a whole different level.

Personal Obedience Prayer

◇◇◇

A journey of obedience question: How are you walking in obedience to God's will in your life right now?
My prayer:

Dear Lord ….

End of Chapter Encouragement

◇◇

Deuteronomy 4:29 (ESV):

"But from there you will seek the Lord your God, and you will find Him, if you search after Him with all your heart and all your soul."

Matthew 13:9, 11–15 (AMP):

He who has ears to hear, let him hear and heed My words.

To you it has been granted to know the mysteries of the Kingdom of Heaven, but to them it has not been granted. For whoever has spiritual wisdom, because he is receptive to God's word, to him more will be given and he will be richly and abundantly supplied; but whoever does not have spiritual wisdom, because he has devalued God's word, even what he has will be taken away from him. Because while having the power of seeing they do not see and while having the power to hearing they do not hear, nor do they understand and grasp spiritual things.

In them the prophecy of Isaiah is being fulfilled, which says:

> "You will hear and keep on hearing, but never understand; and you will look and keep on looking but never comprehend; for this nation's heart has grown hard and with their ears they hardly hear, and they have tightly close their eyes, otherwise they would see with their eyes and hear with their ears and understand with their hearts and turn to me and I would heal them spiritually."

A Journey with the Voice of God

And before the lamp of God went out in the tabernacle of the Lord where the Ark of God was, and while Samuel was lying down, that the Lord called Samuel. And he answered, "Here I am!" So, he ran to Eli and answered, "Here I am, for you called me." And he said, "I did not call; lie down again." And he went and lay down. Then the Lord called yet again, "Samuel!!" So, Samuel arose and went to Eli, and said, "Here I am, for you called me." He answered, "I did not call, my son; lie down again. (Now Samuel did not yet know the Lord, nor was the word of the Lord yet revealed to him.) And the Lord called Samuel again the third time. So, he arose and went to Eli, and said, "Here I am, for you did call me." Then Eli perceived that the Lord had called the boy. Therefore, Eli said to Samuel, "Go, lie down; and it shall be, if He calls you, that you must say, 'Speak, Lord, for Your servant hears.'" So, Samuel went and lay down in his place. Now the Lord came and stood and called as at other times, "Samuel! Samuel!" And Samuel answered, "Speak, for Your servant hears."

—1 Samuel 3:3–10

Have you ever heard the voice of God speaking to you or calling your name?

Oh, I have many times and still do today. I remember one night I wanted to run away from home. That evening, leading up to that, my mom and I had a huge argument. She had said some words that were daggers to my heart. This was in my early teens. I waited until she had gone to bed and was fully asleep and I packed a few of my favorite things into my schoolbag.

I said, "Lord, that is it, I cannot take this no more. Do you see how she speaks to me? Do you hear the words she is using to hurt my heart? And you want me to stay here to put up with this? No way. We fight like Tom and Jerry. You never allow me to answer her back or allow me to speak my mind. It's not fair. It is always children who obey your parents in the Lord, for this is the right thing, so that your days may be long on the earth. Well, what about me, God? What do you say about parents who provoke their children?"

Now, it was around 1:00 A.M. I tiptoed past the bathroom and my mom's bedroom, and down the stairs I went. I put on my jacket and boots because it was freezing cold outside. As I reached to unlock the two locks and chain, I heard, "Don't leave. It is going to be okay. I have it. Do not open that door." My instant reply to what I heard was, "Well, it's too late. I already made up my mind. No more."

It was as though time stood still in those moments as I heard God's voice replying to my action as a young teenager. "Do not leave. I am taking care of it. I promise; just trust me." This reassured my heart a little, but I still wanted to leave. And as I finally opened the front door, my hands could not touch the locks. It was like someone was physically holding me back from pulling the door open.

The voice of God said to me, "Go back upstairs into your room and rest. I will take care of everything. You will see." I was so baffled as to why God was talking me out of leaving, how He blocked me from opening the door and telling me to go and rest. Either way, I obeyed His voice by going back to my room. However, I did leave my schoolbag packed just in case He would change His mind. However, that was what I was hoping for, for Him to see and understand my side. Now, I was unhappy that God had stopped me, but for some reason I was curious. I was curious in wanting to see how He was going to turn all this around for my relationship with my mom.

As believers of the gospel of Jesus Christ, young or old, I realized that no matter what valleys we must sit in or mountains we must face climbing, God is right there every step of the way, guiding us if we are willing to listen and trust Him. There is one thing that we know for sure, and it is this: He may not move when we want Him to. However, we can trust without a doubt that His timing is perfect: He is a God who is never late and never early. He alone holds the blueprint to our lives, just as an architect holds the blueprint in his or her hands for the construction of a building.

You know, for as long as I can remember, I always heard the voice of God talking to me and guiding me. Hearing and following the voice of God growing up was my first nature and still is. No matter where I may be or could be doing, when God has something to say to me, He just says it. God does not need permission to speak to us. Furthermore, He sure does not need to book an appointment to meet with us and our problems. God's schedule is always open for us 24/7, 365 days a year. We do not have to go to a specific place to talk with him; He meets us right where we are. And we are never too young or too old, too high or too low to be able to listen and follow the voice of God.

Our hearts can remain confident in knowing that all the thoughts God has toward us are of peace and not of evil but to give us a future beyond what we know and a hope that we have never experienced before. God's voice will never lead us away from His truth, from His divine peace, or from His presence. And even when we find ourselves walking in the valley of the shadow of death, He is right there with us and guiding us through it all.

Although right now, you may be asking yourself, "Well, how does one hear the voice of God?" or "How do you recognize when it is God speaking and directing you?" Well, for one thing, the voice of God will never contradict the written Word of God, for the thoughts that God has toward us are of peace and unconditional love. It is never of evil but to give us a future and a new hope that we have never experienced before (see Jer. 29:11).

I believe we are all in tune to hear the voice of God, wherever we are and whoever we are with. Now, you might say or think to yourself, "Well, I do not know if I have ever heard the voice of God" or "I am not sure of what His voice sounds like." Better yet, "God never speaks to me." I am sure that at some time or another we have all come to a point in our lives where we have asked and made assumptions. On many occasions I have questioned or even doubted that I heard His voice because of my surroundings and not keeping my focus on God and His Word.

As in the book of 1 Samuel 3:1–10, Samuel heard the voice of God and did not recognize it, but Eli did. In the book of Judges 6:17–22, 36–40, Gideon received a revelation from God, but he was unsure that it was from God so he resorted to asking for a sign three times.

It bears repeating that for as long as I can remember, I have always heard the voice of God speaking to me, directing me, and instructing me.

Long ago in my early teens, there was this specific lady at the church I attended with my mom. For the life of me, I could never remember her name, but her face and stature I will never forget. When she walked into the room, you just knew she was there. I had never spoken to her, and I was never one to speak to anyone around me much, so it was very rare that I would utter a word or sentence in public. However, I had seen her congregate with almost everyone in the church almost every Sunday. Here I was, as always, minding my own business, packing my schoolbag for the morning. And comes the Holy Spirit whispering to me to pray for this lady. My immediate thought and question was "Lord, what do I pray for? What does she need prayer for?"

Now, you may wonder why I would ask that question and why not just pray for her life. Well, as I understood at the time, when someone asks for prayer or you are told to pray for someone, it is important to know what exactly to pray for in their area of need. For example, a person might need prayer for healing with a broken foot, but my prayer for them is for their healing in their nose.

God did not answer my question right away, but instead during the night as I slept. He showed me more than I thought I should know and gave me a personal message to deliver to this lady. As I awoke, every word spoken to me during my sleep I remembered. The question now remained, how on earth was I going to approach this lady and deliver such a message? "I am just a child," I said to myself.

As I continued that week going to school, I muttered in my heart, "Why would you give someone like me such a message to deliver, God? Why would you even choose me to do it? You know I don't like talking to people." All that time I was trying to find a way around not to be the one to deliver the message to this lady. And suddenly, I got this great idea: why not use my mom to tell her about the message for me?

That all sounded like the perfect plan to me while walking home from school. The only problem with that idea was when I asked my mom her reply was no. "No? What you mean no?" I asked. "Well, God chose you to deliver the message, and that is why He gave it to you. He has entrusted it to you and not me for a reason. You are His messenger, so you must be the one to do it. It is up to her what she does with the message; your job is to deliver it," said my mom.

After hearing all of that from my mom, it somewhat encouraged me; however, it did not calm my nerves. That weekend I said to myself (thinking about this lady), "Oh, please don't show up at church." Ha, I figured if she didn't show up, then I would not have to deliver the message. Sunday came, and I am a nervous wreck. Now church did not begin until 3 p.m., which I also questioned. At that time, in my opinion, God would already reach home and sit at the dinner table, eating His dinner after a long day. Those were the thoughts I kept to myself.

Here we are in the service, and of course I looked around and she wasn't there. Inside, I felt somewhat relieved but still concerned. We were about three-quarters of the way into the service, and there she was. But this time around there was no loud entrance. It was more of low-key entrance as though the entire world was on her shoulders. A blind person could see the weight on her, but she tried to put on a brave face during the service. I whispered a prayer for God to give me the courage and strength to deliver the message to her after the service.

As the service came to an end, everyone walked around greeting each other and engaged in conversations. Some loud and some not so loud. As I slowly walked toward her, she was finishing her conversation with another. She turned to me and said, "Hi there, little one."

My reply was, "Hello," and I followed with, "I have a message for you. God told me to tell you this and this is what you will need to do to overcome that situation." After explaining all that was in the message for her, what will happen and what she will need to do to come out on top, this lady looked down on me and told me, "shut up, you know nothing of what you are talking about. You are a child; God would never tell you anything like that or use you. Go sit yourself down."

As a child, can you imagine hearing that? How would that even make you feel? Well, for me, I felt so belittled, ashamed, embarrassed, and hurt. I ran to find my mom, who was serving in the kitchen. The other ladies told me I could not enter at that point, but I did not care; I wanted my mom to stop all that she was doing so that we could leave, after seeing how upset I was, but could not get out of me exactly what happened. We gathered our things to leave, and I had stopped crying; then she asked me, "Did someone say something to you?"

I told her the truth and repeated to her exactly what the lady said to me.

The look on my mom's face changed instantly then she told me, "Do not move from here. I will be right back." As my eyes followed her, I said to myself, "Oh no, why would you go and talk to her?" When I saw my mom reached the lady, I couldn't hear what was being said. However, I saw the hand gesture and her hand pointing to me and the lady looking over toward me. Her facial expression was somewhat of someone warning her and putting her in her place. Then my mom walked away from her, very upset and flustered. She took my hand and put on her jacket, and we headed home.

My mom didn't say anything to me about what had happened until we reached home. I think she also wanted to calm down first before explaining.

"Ayoka, do not allow or let anyone discourage you from delivering any message which God gives you to deliver. It is up to them to do with the message they receive from God. That lady had no right to look down on you like that or speak to you like that. You listen to me, you are a messenger for God, and He chose you for a purpose. God can use anyone to deliver His message. He uses angels, children, and anyone who He sees fit. So just promise me you will continue no matter what, because I can see God using you. Don't doubt his words or the message. And I told her, 'Don't you ever speak to my child like that again, because you won't like it if you try that a second time.' When you see her, don't even look at her; look the other way," said my mom.

After hearing that from my mom, whatever questions I had disappeared. Deep down inside I was still deeply hurt and troubled by the lady's words to me for a very long time. It still does troubles me somewhat in the sense of how many more are out there that share her mindset of "God would never use a child to speak to me." That really left a scar.

During this season in the church they had conventions. This lasted for a few days and would eventually end on a Sunday night. Honestly, I really hated it because it would never finish on time, and we would not get out until almost midnight sometimes. But I did love the fact that there was food to eat. I think that was my only favorite part, sad to say. Do not judge me, because I am just being honest. The food was very good, and there were always different dishes to choose from, but hands down none of them could cook like my mom. She will have you licking your ten fingers when you taste her fried chicken with rice and peas. Any dish she cooks your mouth will be watering, and if you are asleep, the smell alone will wake you up and lead you straight to the pot.

People from neighboring churches and speakers would travel near and far to attend. The dress attire—what can I say? Back then, I would say to myself, "The fashion police needs to come and get them." It made me question everything they were doing and saying.

This lady would never miss any of these conventions; she would come fashionably late with a loud singing entrance.

From that Sunday and the encounter I had with her, no one had heard from her nor seen her. No one knew where she was and what happened to her. Week after week, then months after months, and then just over a year and a half.

This Sunday, I sat in the corner, looking out of the window with my thoughts to God. And the side door opened as a member was in the middle of giving their testimony. There she was the lady had returned with a grand entrance with a worship song and praise in her heart.

Oh, I immediately sank down so low in my chair. If the chair could swallow me up, I would allow it just to be invisible. My heart began beating so fast, my mind racing and thinking of ways just to exit without the lady seeing me. I looked over to see where my mom was, and as she looked over toward me; she could tell what was going on inside of me.

No sooner after the pastor got the mic from a member who was giving a testimony, he asked if there was anyone else wanting to give a testimony before he started the message. The lady jumped up and said, "Praise the Lord church!" and started singing a song, which the rest of the church joined in.

Could you picture me sitting in that little corner, begging this chair to swallow me up without moving a muscle? Well, that was the case, I started praying in my heart that this lady would not remember me or much less see me.

After she finished singing, she stood at the front and greeted the pastor. She went on to tell the church about the storms she had been going through and how she almost did not make it through and when she had lost it all and there was no way out around her. The Holy Spirit brought back to her memory the face of this child who God had sent to her and warned her of the storms and what she would need to do to overcome it. So, when she remembered the message and applied it, everything began to turn around for her. But she also remembered how she treated the vessel who God chose to deliver her message because of her pride.

As she continued sharing, I was at war with myself and God within. My mind was racing with questions. Sitting there, I said to God, "Please, do not let her approach me; she still has nothing to say to me. She can just tell you sorry, God." Deep down within, I was happy that she made it through what God had shown me.

No sooner had the service finished than I grabbed my Bible and jacket and glued myself to my mom's side. My mom knew why I did that. The lady started making her way over to where my mom and I were, and immediately I positioned myself behind my mom and began shadowing her steps.

She greeted my mom with a humbling smile. My mom was very polite, and she asked my mom if she could have a word with me.

As my mom turned around to ask me, I was already shaking my head no, so my mom said, "It is okay. I am not going anywhere. I am standing right here." She then turned to the lady and told her, "Whatever you have to say to my daughter you can say it to me, and she can hear you."

The lady humbly started off by saying, "I am so sorry for the way that I spoke to you and treated you. I asked God for help, and He sent me the answer through a child, and I was arrogant in my own ways. But God used you to teach me a lesson, and everything He shared with you happened, and the instructions which He gave you to give me I remembered at the end, and everything turned around and saved my life. So, I just want to say thank you, and I hope that you continue to do as God leads you. Please accept my apology."

I did not know how to react or what exactly to say. I only said, "It's okay" while clinging onto my mom's hip. She then reached over to hand me a British five-pound note. However, I refused to take it from her. My mom then also told her, "No, thank you, it is okay; my daughter doesn't like taking things from anyone, but she accepted your apology."

Being a young witness to this did in many ways build my faith deeper in God, my faith in knowing and believing that God never gets it wrong. And I can trust in all that He speaks and shares with me. Now, perhaps it was not their season to understand but rather to strengthen their faith in how God would prove Himself to them.

Sometimes God uses someone who you least expect to give you a word or an answer to what you have been asking or waiting on God for. Be careful how and who you dismiss because it could just be a message for you. Do not be so quick to dismiss the unexpected person who God has chosen to deliver His message to you, but do have the discernment of the spirit to know that it is indeed a spiritual word for you.

> "Teach me good judgment (discernment) and knowledge, for I have believed and trusted and relied on Your commandments" (Ps. 119:66).

> "Hear, O children, the instruction of a father and pay attention and be willing to learn so that you may gain understanding and intelligent discernment" (Prov. 4:1).

> "For God did not give us a spirit of timidity or cowardice or fear, but He gave us a spirit of power and of love and of sound judgment and personal discipline abilities that result in a calm, well-balanced mind and self-control" (2 Tim. 1:7, AMP).

I remember there was a season I was going through while living in London. This season was very hard, and everything I tried was met with a brick wall. This specific afternoon I was off from college and work. There I was in my room, a little stressed out to the point where I began to cry. The more I cried, the more my anger arose in me.

"God, why, why me? Why can't you just answer me? What do you want from me? Look at me, why do I have to be going through so much? Why do you keep making this hard? You make it easy for others. What is the point of any of this, huh, what is the point?"

"Keep asking, and it will be given to you; keep seeking, and you will find; keep knocking, and the door will be opened to you. For everyone who keeps asking receives; he who keeps seeking finds; and to him who keeps knocking, the door will be opened." (Matt. 7:7–8).

In the middle of my venting and shouting at God, unwilling to calm down, God knew exactly what to do because He was already ahead of me. He knew the desires that were in my heart. He knew the pain that I was carrying. He had a word for me during the middle of my storm, and He needed it to reach me in a way that I could never doubt that it was not Him.

The messenger whom He chose took me off guard. But it was someone He knew I would be willing to meet up with and listen to what she was instructed to share with me. There were a few things I shared with God in my room that day while crying. And there were three questions that I asked.

To my surprise, God not only revealed my questions but also gave her the answer to the questions.

As my friend began to share with me all that the Lord had revealed to her about my situation, the hair on the back of my neck stood up. And this sudden reassurance gave me the confidence to continue my journey with Him. Now I can testify to you that two out of those three questions have been fully answered. The first one was answered a few years ago, just as God said it would. And the second one came to past recently.

The second one took me a while to realize. It was not until the Holy Spirit had me ministering to a friend, and in the middle of the Word,

I was reminded of my own request and how it was answered. That is two out of three! Now the third one does require God's divine perfect timing as always.

If ever you want to remember anything, please remember this: if the word/message is from God, It will always come to pass, but if the word is from man, it shall surely fall to the ground.

The Word of God will never fail you. The only word that can fail you if you place your faith and hopes in it is man's word.

> For the word of God is living and active and full of power making it operative, energizing, and effective. It is sharper than any two-edged sword, even penetrating as far as the division of soul and spirit, of both joints and marrow, and able to judge the thoughts and intentions of the heart.
>
> —Ephesians 4:12

Man's promises are empty. But God's promises are everlasting.

> "Your kingdom is an everlasting kingdom, And Your dominion endures throughout all generations. The Lord is faithful in His words, And holy in all His works" (Ps. 145:13)

If man had given me those promises that I had placed in God's hands, I most definitely would have doubted them and more so had questions on top of questions. But God knew the deep, longing desires of my heart. He knew the time, the place, and the vessel to use just to get my attention, thereby giving me a deeper confidence in Him, to know without a doubt that it was Him and that He heard my cry.

Who is this King of glory, mighty and strong in battle, who knows my thoughts before I think them? I cannot say that I know the mind of God. None of us knows the mind of God except the Spirit of God. We look on a person, and yet truly we do not know their mind but only some of their thoughts they may share with us.

> "Who is the King of glory? The Lord strong and mighty, the Lord mighty in battle." (Ps. 24:8).

This reminds me of my college days. My close friends always used to say to me, "Oh my gosh, you are like an onion. You have so many layers. You only allow who you want to let close to see a different layer."

I do not know if I should have taken that as a compliment or question them about it. However, deep down inside, I began over the years seeing what they meant by that description. To know the mind of a man, you must also know the spirit of a man, which I believe is a hard rock. If that individual trusts you enough, they might, but if not, you will only see what they allow you to see. We must be extremely careful in how and what we share from our hearts to those around us because not everyone who surrounds us are for us or supports what God has placed within us.

> "Watch over your heart with all diligence, for from it flow the springs of life." (Prov. 4:23).

> "'For I know the plans that I have for you,' declares the Lord, 'plans for prosperity and not for disaster, to give you a future and a hope.'" (Jer. 29:11).

> For what person knows the thoughts and motives of a man except the man's spirit within him? So also no one knows the thoughts of God except the Spirit of God. Now we have received, not the spirit of the world, but the Holy Spirit who is from God, so that we may know and understand the wonderful things freely given to us

by God. We also speak of these things, not in words taught or supplied by human wisdom, but in those taught by the Spirit, combining, and interpreting spiritual thoughts with spiritual words for those being guided by the Holy Spirit.

—2 Corinthians 2:11–13

Here I am, frustrated, and my mind overwhelmed. Better yet, my entire spirit is at war with God. I feel so done with everything and everyone around me. Perhaps I just need to disappear from everyone, and they just might notice I am no longer around to be milked dry. Okay, so maybe I am just overthinking too much, but my heart deeply feels at war with God.

Another year, and it is that time of year again, it's fast approaching. Whoop, whoop Easter Camp. I used to look forward to going every year, but for some reason I just do not feel excited anymore. I really do not need to be there this year; they can do without me, plus they have enough volunteers. Well, that is what I told myself, trying to talk myself out of having anything to do with camp.

Oh gosh, it is Sunday, maybe if I try to avoid my youth pastor, he will be distracted enough with all the parents and applications, and he will not notice I haven't filled out anything or agreed to help this year. The best I will do is sponsor two youths who cannot afford to go. After all, I remember my very first camp and how my life was changed by it, so why not? Whoever they are, they will have a life-changing experience.

Great, a large crowd walking out the doors; church is over, and I am trying to mix in the crowd to go straight to the exit doors. Nope, that did not work, was he looking out just to see if he spotted me? "Darn it," I said to myself. "Ayoka, hold on!" I turned and gave a smile to pretend I am in a hurry, but that did not work. My youth pastor was already in front of me. "Hi, how are you? I did not see you come to the interest meeting. And I was looking forward to your application. Didn't you get one?"

Now, if you know me well and are super close to me, you know that I cannot lie because the moment I try to lie my face gives me away and I am smiling all the way to Timbuktu. So, I saw how intent his questions were and I simply said, "Well, you know this year I wasn't planning on attending; however, I can sponsor two youth to attend." Me thinking that would also give me a pass, and that would be enough. "What? What do you mean you're skipping this year of Easter camp? Oh no, we need you. You must come; you did such an awesome job last year, and I need you back in that position. No one else can do it like you. I have an application for you, and I will fill it out, but you must come. We have a meeting on Saturday at Spencer Place. It starts at nine a.m. I need to see you there, okay?"

Here I am still trying to convince my youth pastor of another reason I cannot attend. "You know, I have not requested time off from work in advance for camp. And camp is three weeks away. I really do not believe with such short notice that they will give me a week off."

Ha, you all thought that excuse worked? Nope. "I believe they will, and I will see you this Saturday morning for the meeting. I will see you then. Let me go and finish with these parents who have been waiting to talk with me."

Now, I am even more mad at myself because he really is expecting me at that meeting. I am working Friday night until Saturday morning. That means when I leave work, I must freshen up and go straight to this meeting that I really do not want to go to nor serve at camp this year. Yes, you may be asking, then why you would go even though you do not want to? Why not just put your foot down and say no?

Well, first I am at war with God and at war with myself. Remember, even though I am at war with God, He is still God, and I fear Him. Fear as in reverence Him because deep within there is just a tugging within my spirit gently nudging me to go, and I am trying to fight it. In other words, I am trying to be disobedient to this prompting in my spirit.

Can I tell you that even during chaos around us and within us, God can and still speaks to us through His still small voice inside of our hearts.

The next stop is mine, so I rang the bell and got off the bus. It is only a three-minute walk, but why does it feel so long? I am thinking, "I really do not want to serve for an entire week. It just feels like a circle; what do I even get from it? Nothing, I watch and see how everyone gets their breakthroughs, and I am happy for them—I truly am. But it just feels like all I have been doing is live to work and work to live. I get up, I go to work, I go home, I sleep, I eat, I go to church, I serve, I smile, I go home and begin the entire process again. I am tired of it all—something must change. Isn't there more to life than this, God? You have me here and yet you are not using me. Why? Why do you still have me in this place? What is the purpose? Why do I still feel stuck in all of this? There must be more out there."

I have had people say to me, "You know, talking to yourself is the first sign of madness." But my reply to them would be, "Nope, talking to myself is not the first sign of madness. It is answering myself." That would always leave them laughing and walking away from me.

> "Come to me, all of you who are struggling and burdened, and I will give you rest. Take my yoke upon you and learn from me, because I am gentle and humble in heart, and you will find rest for your souls. For my yoke is easy, and my burden is light" (Matt. 11:28–30).

No, I was not talking to myself, while walking to the meeting place. Even though I was angry and frustrated at God, I found myself sharing some of what was already on my mind, which He already knew, but He did say, "Come as I am," so that was what I was doing.

God is a great listener; I know He was listening intently even though I wanted Him to say something.

> "He will listen to the prayers of the destitute, for he is never too busy to heed their requests." (Ps. 102:17, TLB).

Wow, there are a lot of servant leaders here already, and everything is set up. All the chairs are set in a huge circle, which to me means we will be seeing everyone's face. I just want this all finished, I told myself.

Suddenly, the youth pastor clapped his hands and said, "Right. Let us begin with prayer. We are praying for all the youth who will be attending, for their families, protection, praying for the journey, praying for the campgrounds and their staff, we are praying for all the volunteers and leaders and for God to ready our hearts and minds. Okay!"

Everyone is now walking around the room, some praying out-loud and others praying quietly. As I walked around myself, I looked around the room and asked, "Lord, why do you even have me here? You know I am not in the mood to serve, and You already know my heart."

Then out of nowhere I heard our youth pastor's voice, and I looked up toward his direction. It is as though he was crying because the Holy Spirit was moving within him. "God says this year at camp will be different. This year, He wants us to just come and serve. All the other years we always go to expect and take. But this year He wants us to just go and serve His children without asking in return for anything. Because He knows our needs, but this is not about us as leaders, it is about the youth who we are serving. Just serve, that is it," he said, as he wiped the tears from his eyes. Darn it, it seems as though I was crying too because I knew that was not Him speaking to us. I quietly said in my heart before sitting down, "Fine, serve, you say, and not ask for anything in return. That is what I will do. That is fine by me; I am not going to ask for anything."

After all the formalities of the meeting and important paperwork we all had to sign, it seems it is official that I was off to camp again. As I got ready to leave, my youth leader gave me a hug and said, "Thank you. This year is going to be great, and I trust that you will be great at camp coordinator."

Personally, I as though God was setting me up. I just could not put my finger on how, but for Him to use our youth pastor to say, "Just come to serve" somehow just stuck with me for the rest of the week leading up to camp.

Somehow, I pushed my anger and frustration from the forefront of my mind and told myself, "Just serve, that's all, nothing more and nothing less, but give my all in serving." As I looked around on the coach everyone was super hyped, the laughter, taking selfies and making new friends. I was happy for them because I knew those feelings all too well. But for me this year I just could not shake off the heaviness I was feeling deep within. This longing and this hunger for something different, for more, just more, and no more of the same old, same old.

Oh yes, there is that smell of fresh air mixed with horses, cows, and all the other farm animal manure. Yep, we are here, far away from the city, and now out in the countryside surrounded by farms. I remember when we first came here. Oh my gosh, I could not stand the smell of all that fresh manure in the early mornings. But now I have learned to appreciate it with the amazing sunrise, the stillness of peace, and seeing the mist on the grass. It is just beautiful and peaceful; most importantly, you can hear your thoughts as you walk about the grounds.

A few of the leaders got here before we set up the heavy stuff, and that includes the sound system and band. Well, here we go, I told myself. I did not have to worry about my camp bag because some of the leaders who were waiting for the coaches to arrive took all our bags to the gym and along with the letter coach. This made it easier for us all to find our bags later when assigned our group blocks and rooms.

After saying hi to a few youths who were all on cloud nine, I headed to my section to set up just outside the worship hall, a point of reference for anyone who needed to know where to go; it lets them know which rooms needed what for that specific workshop, for any lost and found and extra materials like first aid or if someone just wanted to take a moment out.

As I began to set up my table, all I kept reminding myself of was, "Just serve nothing more and nothing less, just give your all and not ask the Lord for anything." So, I poured out everything within me on the first night, making sure alongside the other leaders that everything was all in order for the next day. The first night was a tremendous success, and the energy in worship was one never to forget.

Now comes the fun part, separating all the campers. All boys to the right section of the building, and all girls to the left. The great part about that setup was for either group to get to each other, they would have to come to the center of the building, where my table was set up, where the worship hall and the dining room were. There was no escape to either side without being caught when it was room time and lights out. There were also six to seven leaders, and out of them there would be two who are overall in charge, while the others would be assigned a few youths to oversee and be a point of reference for.

Toward the end of our first evening there, I found out in which block and room I was staying. Furthermore, I also found out that one of the youths who I had sponsored was also sharing rooms with myself and two others. It was okay because she did not know anyone there apart from me; after all, I did invite her. My hope was that she would be able to make long-lasting friends with the others and find her way.

The second day was a full, packed day; it was a full-on serving day, which was for sure. I had not touched base with any of my close friends there. Well, they too were busy serving; however, I did make efforts to check on how they were doing and if they needed my help with anything.

Now we were halfway through camp. It is Wednesday, and I have a slight break in between the breakout sections before lunch. I sat there at the table and started to evaluate how none of my close friends and I had not met up to even chat with each other. Are things changing between us all? What was going on, and why does everything feel so distant among us all?

It was lunch time, and the youths began to enter the lunch hall slowly. I was touched by a few of the youths passing by me. Many just wanted a hug from me or just wave with a warm smile of acknowledgment. Somehow, I still was not sure how all of this was pouring out of me, but God knows because within, I was still hurting and very much torn.

After lunch, during the outdoor activities, I convinced myself to go and walk about while snapping pictures of the excitement and fears on their faces when they were on the obstacles. Seeing how the other youths on the ground would cheer the ones who were climbing or hanging from the tower and zipline made me smile with joy. A handful of them spotted me, they tried to convince me to join them by climbing the tower to leap off the top and grab the triangle. All that excitement at the time did not work with their persistence and trying to make deals with me if I did it, they give me or do for me.

I gave in to them in the end because they had promised that the next day they would come for me again. Here I am, climbing this tower with one of the youths who was petrified. However, though she had this fear, she just wanted me to climb with her so she could get over her fear of heights. I saw how she had this trust in her, this confidence and belief that if I climbed with her, she would be okay and could do it.

Who was I to deny her and crush her faith, trust, and confidence? And then I was reminded in my spirit what our youth pastor had shared in the meeting before the camp: "Just serve His children. We are there for them. They are the next generation." So, I looked all the way up to the top of that swaying tower feeling the strong wind, telling myself, "Well, show no fear; this is for her to get to the top." If I told you I was not scared myself, I would surely be lying. But somehow this youth had so much faith and confidence in me to climb with her, that it would help her get to the top. So now I cannot let her down, and I believed in her to get up there.

> "But Jesus said, 'Leave the children alone, and do not forbid them to come to Me; for the kingdom of heaven belongs to such as these'" (Matt. 19:14).

We were halfway to the top, and well, the wind picked up even more. Truly I wanted to go back down, but when I heard her say, "Okay, I am scared. I want to go back down now. I cannot do it," my own fear snapped within, and I began to encourage her that we must finish. We had climbed this far, and it was now a long way down. "Come on, let us go, you did not have me climb with you not to reach the top. We are doing this together; let us go." Suddenly, we both began hearing all the cheering from the ground from the others looking up. I took a tiny peek and saw that there was a way larger crowd than when we started climbing, and now a lot of the senior leaders were also cheering us both on. And suddenly what seemed impossible became possible. She did it. She is now standing on the top of the tower and getting ready to jump.

> "At that time the disciples came to Jesus and said, 'Who then is greatest in the kingdom of heaven?' And He called a child to Himself and set him among them, and said, 'Truly I say to you, unless you change and become like children, you will not enter the kingdom of heaven. So, whoever will humble himself like this child, he is the greatest in the kingdom of heaven. And whoever receives one such child in My name, receives Me'" (Matt. 18:1–5).

In my mind I told myself, "It's okay, I do not need to get to the top, I was only pushing myself so that she would reach the top." Then her voice interrupted my thoughts, "Come on, hurry up. I want us to jump together!" My reply: "No, it's okay. You go." But she was not having it, and the cheer from the others below us got even louder.

Yes, I made it to the top, and we both counted one, two, three, and then jumped. You would have thought we won the Olympics with all the cheering of joy from below. Finally, we were both lowered down. The joy and random celebration with everyone hugging us is unforgettable. They witnessed our journey in climbing that tower and could see the struggle with the natural eyes, and their spirit knew our spiritual struggle and there by shouting for joy for victory before we made it to the top. It was profound because that celebration sounded out the trumpets, causing both of our fears to fall off like scales.

As I looked over to the youth who I climbed with, she was full of so much light and was already encouraging another that they too can do it. My heart was happy for her in every way.

After I met up with a fewof the other leaders for a meeting before the service, it was shared to me that what I did meant a lot to that specific youth because since we had all got to camp, she saw that obstacle and feared it the most. I said, "Well, it was my pleasure to be of service to her even though she did not know I was more scared than her."

Isn't it amazing to see the young body of Christ coming together and growing like this? This was already an experience that had left an imprint on my heart. Could this have beenmy one highlight for just being here to serve, I asked myself.

As we all went back to the building to freshen up for dinner and then service, I was still amazed at the fact of the tower, the wind, the fears, and the victory that had come out of it; all of which I was not ready for or rather, expecting. Now service was about to begin, and it seems as though this time around we did not have rounding up to do for the youths. They were all ready with such exciting energy to enter praise and worship. I even saw more of the young males with their Bibles walking, giving high-fives.

Something seems to be quite different with the atmosphere tonight, and it is only Wednesday night. Wow. The worship, the message was on a deeper level. The Spirit of God was seriously moving right before our very own eyes. Youths are going up to the altar, surrendering all and confessing that Jesus Christ is Lord. They fell on their knees in worship and was crying. "They are truly surrounded by the precious love of God," I said to myself. Thank you, Lord, for allowing me to see this, even though I have not asked you for anything.

> "Seek the Lord while He may be found; Call upon Him while He is near" (Isa. 55:6).
>
> Praise the Lord! Praise God in His sanctuary; Praise Him in His mighty expanse.
>
> Praise Him for His mighty deeds; Praise Him according to His excellent greatness. Praise Him with trumpet sound; Praise Him with harp and lyre. Praise Him with tambourine and dancing;
>
> Praise Him with stringed instruments and flute. Praise Him with loud cymbals;
>
> Praise Him with resounding cymbals. Everything that has breath shall praise the Lord.
>
> Praise the Lord!
>
> —Psalm 150

After service ended with a praise song, the love in the atmosphere was stronger than what the enemy thought he could manage. Youths who had issues with each other or who were in gangs came together in unity under Christ, with forgiveness for each other's offences, lifting and praying for each other. There was no denying that God's presence was not among us all and on this camp. I lost count of the hugs I received from so many youths of both sides.

> Shout joyfully to the Lord, all the earth. Serve the Lord with jubilation; Come before Him with rejoicing. Know that the Lord Himself is God; It is He who has made us, and not we ourselves; We are His people and the sheep of His pasture. Enter His gates with thanksgiving, And His courtyards with praise. Give thanks to Him, bless His name. For the Lord is good; His mercy is everlasting, and His faithfulness is to all generations.
>
> —Psalm 100

Cleaning up was not an issue, and getting everyone back to their blocks was too easy. They all helped the leaders to set up for the next day. After all the youths went back to their blocks, a few of us leaders were still in the communal area going through a few this of how light the next day would be because there would be a talent showcase for what each workshop had been working on.

Also, they would be presenting it all in the service, and in the evening, there will be an award service for outstanding youths. After the rundown, a few of us leaders stayed behind until midnight. All the youth should be fast asleep by now; well, that was what we said to each other and then said good night. While walking down the corridor in my block to my room, I said to myself, "Okay, try not to wake the others. Your main mission is put your stuff down and go straight to the shower and then bed. You are lucky if you get six hours sleep, so no time to waste."

"Ha, ha, ha." The moment I turned the key in the door and opened, the youth who I had sponsored rushed up to me in extreme excitement. Whatever high energy she was on, I had no match for such because I was feeling exhausted, and all that was left on my mind was a shower and sleep. So, I mentioned what I had come to do and asked why she was not already asleep because lights are out at 11:00 P.M.

As she continued explaining, I had already grabbed my towel and stood in front of the bathroom door ready to close it and tell her just go to bed. But she just kept going on and on with such a fire. So, I said, "Okay, okay, fine. Can you just let me get in the shower for ten minutes? When I get out, I will listen to you sing the song which the Holy Spirit gave you to write in your workshop. Is that okay? Because it has been a very long day." To my surprise she was okay with my request.

> Even today my complaint is rebellion; His hand is heavy despite my groaning. Oh, that I knew how to find Him, That I might come to His home! I would present my case before Him And fill my mouth with arguments. I would learn the words which He would answer And perceive what He would tell me. Would He contend with me by the greatness of His power? No, surely, He would pay attention to me. There the upright would argue with Him; And I would be free of my Judge forever.
>
> —Job 23

I stood under the warm shower, hoping that by the time I had finished she would have already went to bed and fell asleep. I purposely took more than 10 minutes. What if I told you all, this young lady stood waiting outside the bathroom for me to come out so that she could practice singing the song she wrote? Well, guess what? She surely did.

No sooner had I finished and wrapped myself up in my towel, unlocked the bathroom door and came out than she was standing right in my face, smiling, and asking if I was ready to hear it. Through my annoyance, I told her, "Sure, sure, sing it." As she backed up next to one of the beds, I stood still with my towel wrapped around and dripping. She began to sing!

Within the first word of the first line on the first verse, I could not move from the spot where I stood. The words were like daggers entering my chest, my heart, and my spirit that I fell on my knees and then to my face. I was crying beyond my physical tears from a depth I have never felt before. The more she sang the words to this song, the more I felt as though I was being sliced in pieces and was held in the very presence of God Himself. I could not stop crying if I wanted to nor be able to get up when I tried.

As I looked up to try and get her to stop singing, her eyes were closed and I could not stop her. By now it was already 30 minutes later, and she was still singing, and I was still crying. Now one of my other friends who was also sharing rooms with us came in and came straight to me on the floor. "Ayoka, hun, what is wrong? What is going on, I've never seen you cry like this. It is okay, just talk to me, please." I heard her, but somehow, I could not respond to her. Then I heard somebody told her, "Don't touch her; just sit on the floor until she is able to stand."

Then, suddenly, I heard the voice of God, clearly: "My child, I need you to surrender to Me. Allow Me to break you."

"What do You mean broken? Why would you break me? You can use me just as I am, Lord. I do not want to be broken. Just use me as I am!" I replied.

"My child, I need you broken, I need you to surrender so I can break you to use you. Just allow me to break you," the voice of God said to me.

"No, no, I do not want to be broken. Use me just as I am; you do not need to break me. I just want to stop crying and get up from this floor!" I said to the voice of God.

"I cannot allow you to get up until you allow me to break you. You cannot get up until you allow me to break you!' He replied. Then I tried pushing myself up off the floor and as I did, my back met with this hand half the size of my back, blocking me from rising from the floor.

"No, I want to get up. If I must fight You, I will all night. I do not want to be crying anymore," I said to the voice of God.

"My child, I cannot allow you to get up until you allow Me to break you!"

By this time, I had been on the floor crying for what felt like forever, but was only two hours. This young lady was still singing, and my friend was still sitting on the floor next to me, singing along. She was also listening to what I was saying, but for sure she was wondering why I was saying what I was muttering aloud.

I began to feel very weak, and all that strength that I had been fighting with God to allow me to get up from the floor without surrendering to His will. Suddenly, I had no more fight left in me to fight Him or argue with Him anymore. Now I am starting to understand what Jacob felt when he was wrestling with the angel of the Lord for that blessing.

"Fine, fine, break me. Is that what You want? Here I am. I surrender. Just break me. I surrender it all; take all of it. Just take it all; break me as You will. I am done fighting You!" I said to Him as my face was still on the floor.

"Thank you. Now I can use you," the voice of God said to me. Immediately after, I was able to get off the floor. My friend helped me up and walked me over to my bed so I could sit. Would you believe I was on the floor for over three hours, crying and fighting with God? There was an exceptionally large patch on the carpet soaked with tears, maybe the size of an eight-inch pizza.

In the next three and a half hours, I must be up for morning prayer with our leaders and then come back and get ready for breakfast. I lay on my bed, just looking out the window, not lost but just at a loss for words to describe the encounter I had with God, so much so that I could never deny Him. And then I thought to myself, "Are You serious? In my towel?"

After closing my eyes, the time went so fast because I heard my alarm. I do not believe I slept at all, I told myself. As I went into the bathroom to brush my teeth, I took a moment to look in the mirror. And my oh my, my eyes were as puffed up as if they had been stung by a bee. You know I had to find my sunglasses to wear for the rest of the day.

Returning to my room, I had to wake up the others so that they did not miss the breakfast cutoff. To my surprise, the young lady who sang said she wanted to tell me something. So, I smiled at her and said, "Sure. What is it?"

"I don't think I can sing that song anymore in worship after seeing what happened to you last night while I was singing. I don't want anyone else to be hurt by it."

I was not expecting that at all. I looked her in the eyes and told her, "What happened to me is that God needed to have an encounter with me. He had to bring me face down, and He spoke to me. Your singing did not hurt me. God used you and gave you these words to write. He gave it to you to sing; it is breaking strongholds and setting those free from their bondage. Please, please, you must sing this song in morning worship. I promise you that I am not hurt; rather, on the other hand, I am beyond words and blessed. So, thank you for sharing it with me last night. Do not fear in singing this song; you will see how God uses it this morning to bring everyone to their knees. Trust me!"

Eventually we all left to get breakfast, and then myself and some of the other leaders started gathering everyone for praise and worship. I felt as though I was walking on air. And within me was this empty, but on a different level, as though there were another dimension of emptiness and that was where God had taken me when I allowed Him to break me. I not only felt different, but I also looked different inside and out.

Everyone was now in the worship hall. Personally, I wanted to just stand at the back on the inside of the doorway. I just knew within what was about to come upon everyone in the room like what I had experienced hours prior. I was excited within, and as I looked over to my right side, a friend I was once really close with finally acknowledged me. She walked over and had a very curious look, then asking, "Are you okay? I have not seen you most of camp. Why do you look so different? Something is different about how you look. I do not know what it is. But hey, I am sorry for not talking with you the entire camp."

I looked at her with such peace, forgiveness, and love like I had never known. "It's okay, I am more than good, and everything was okay." For the life of me, I really could not remember what I had to forgive her about or anything else. The one thing that I knew for sure was that God had taken it all. All from my heart and from my mind and from my spirit. I was no longer weighed down by any thoughts nor feeling that was not of God. I gave her a hug to affirm what I said, and she went to find her seat.

As praise and worship finished, the young lady got invited up to sing the song. As they got her mic ready, she looked at me standing at the back. I could only smile and give her a thumbs up, to encouraged her that it was going to be wonderful. I am not sure why I was the only one standing at the back at that time while everyone else sat, but God knew.

I heard some of the whispers, "Wait, she can sing?" "I didn't know she could sing!" I smiled yet again to myself secretly saying, "You just don't know what is about to happen."

As she began to sing, there was immediate stillness in the entire room. First, one and then two youths stood up, and then the youth pastor and his wife, then our main church pastor and his wife, and everyone else who had been seated arose to their feet. With their hands raised, the Spirit of God showered over the room like a rushing wind. And all I saw was every single person on the floor. From the members of the worship team to the ones working on techs. They were all on the floor in tears, face down, on their knees, crying and crying in the presence of God. As that young lady was the only one left on the stage singing in unison with the presence of God, I could only smile, smile because I knew what was happening and how they were feeling in His presence. Well, more of the process, while standing at the back and looking across the room just in awe and joy for everyone and what God was also doing for them like what He did for me.

Anything else that was planned for that day was no longer a priority or was that important. To be able to see God's presence bring everyone to their knees, no matter your title or age or position like that was beyond everything I thought I knew about God. Even a few of the workers of the campground came in to see what was happening, and they too fell to their knees in His presence and began crying.

Some of us have this posh or cute cry. This crying was not one of those. This was in the presence of the King of kings and Lord of lords. We were all in His presence, just as we were, even if you had plastered your face with makeup and the whole nine yards, all of that would have been stripped away with the tears. Whatever and whoever God needed to set free, heal, or whoever needed forgiveness and deliverance, all was being done at that very moment and more. Pastors, leaders, youths, and workers were all in the presence of God.

Everything was different, and nothing was ever the same. There was a great shifting from God. Chains fell off places we never knew were there. Testimonies came forth as though a riverbank burst open. I am not talking about meaningless things here. I am talking about life and death situations. Things you might not have ever considered these young teenagers could ever experience but would be so fast to place a label and judgment on based on their behavior.

Have you ever heard the saying "Never judge a book by its cover?" Well, this was that very moment. The testimonies from abandonment, abuse, brokenness, feeling unloved, addictions, gang-related loss of friends, no family, suicidal thoughts, healing from sickness, and more. Could you really bring your minds around to the reality that as much as you have seen these youth smile, joke around, make you laugh, and show you their many talents? Could you imagine that deep down they are going through a ragging storm, at home, at school, maybe church, with their parent/guardian, or at a foster home?

Some of us honestly never gave it a thought because we think it is not on our doorstep. Or rather, everything is peachy with the youth you know. Can I tell you they could be the very ones who need your help and time the most. Just your ear and not your judgment of their lifestyle because you do not know the pain or shame they must carry.

My heart was truly overwhelmed hearing all these testimonies from the youths with such boldness and courage strengthened by God to stand in front of their peers to declare what they have been healed from or set free from and what God has shown them and how they have felt His love and touch.

There is no way you can convince me that God is not present in your life if your eyes are not on Him or seeking just to sit at His feet. These youths had nothing to lose by seeking God but everything to gain, and so do you and me.

Now there was this one youth for whom it was her very first time. She has two older brothers who always came, but she was too young until this particular year. From a young age she had been battling an illness, which would keep her out of school for long periods of time and into the hospital. She testified to the fact of how she had always relied on her mother's faith in God for her to be healed and how she always wanted this one person to come and visited her while she was in the hospital to keep her company because she felt more peace. She said, "As I was just on the floor crying, God told me that I must believe in Him myself for my own healing. And that my parents' faith can only take me so far. But now is the time to believe for my own healing, now! I told Him that I do believe in Him and for my healing and that I did not want to believe through my parents anymore. Then He told me that I was fully healed and to just thank Him."

As she spoke those words with tears running down her cheeks, she shouted from the top of her lungs, declaring that sickness no longer had a hold on her, her life, or her trust in God. "And if you want Him to heal you too from whatever it is, I dare you to believe in Him! Because I believe and I am not going to doubt what He has told me, no matter what anyone or the doctors say!"

I stood in awe at her testimony with tears filling my eyes. I did not know I had any left in me to cry. I remember her but when she was much smaller. Her mom used to call me and told me that she was asking for me. She wanted me to come and visit her on the children's ward, which was the same hospital that my mother works at.

I was taken back because she was requesting for me to visit. And what she did not know is I have a thing about visiting hospitals and not wanting to be in any. However, my mother said, "You know that children always have a sixth sense about someone, and if they take a liking to you, that is it. So, there is nothing wrong with you visiting; maybe she just wants your company." Now, my work schedule was conflicting with visiting time at the hospital. So, I went ahead and requested morning shifts, which I totally hated only because I love to sleep in. However, this was for an important cause. So, as soon as I got off work, I would change out of my work clothes and head straight to the hospital and along the way, bring a few treats that I thought she may enjoy.

This was no longer Sunday school, I told myself. And this would be the first time I would see her outside of Sunday school. I had to just suck it all up of how I feel about hospitals and the thought of being in one just for her. I informed her mother that I would visit that day because she has had not stop asking for me to visit, so I really did not want to disappoint her. I was not sure what to expect or what exactly I would do, but I told myself, "Just stay for an hour or so and then head home to get some rest."

To my surprise, she was not having a good day, and her nurses were trying their hardest to keep her in high spirits and trying to tell her jokes, but she just was not having it. As I stood outside her room door watching and listening, I popped my head around the corner and smiled. Her entire face lit up, and her energy went from zero to a hundred, and the nurses had to remind her to take it easy because she was physically weak.

I called her mom to let her know that I was there, and she asked if I could wait until she got there before leaving, and I agreed. But when the little one found out her mom was on the way, she took the phone and told her it is okay, she didn't need to come because I was there. She could come tomorrow. To myself, I was wondering, "Why would you tell your mom that, and why are you so excited that I am here with you?"

She was so excited that I had to go on a tour to the play area on her ward, and she really did not want her nurses to interrupt her time with me. We watched movies and played with all kinds of toys that were available there. Once or twice, I asked if she wanted to take a break, but she refused. After seeing the time, I hinted that I would have to leave soon. Upon hearing that from me, suddenly that bright spark began to dim extremely fast. Then the silence, so I asked, "Hey, what is wrong? What are you thinking about?"

"I really do not want you to go yet. I really want you to stay longer and play with me. The doctors and nurses are too busy to really have fun time with me. I have not been to school in a while because I always have to be here because of this disease that keeps on attacking my body. I know mommy says that one day I will be healed. But when? Why can't God heal me now? And because I am hardly at school, I do not have any friends there. You are always kind to me and give me hugs at church, so I asked mom if she could ask you to visit me."

Upon hearing all of that in one mouthful, I had to fight back my tears. There was no other option but to remain for a few more hours until visiting time was over. Visiting her often during that hard season in her younger years not only blessed her but also blessed me in more ways than one. Because here I am standing, and she is thirteen years of age at camp, standing in front of a hundred-plus older youths testifying that she is healed because God told her so.

"What am I truly witnessing here, God? Why are you allowing me to witness all of this?" I asked.

Upon leaving camp on Friday, the following Sunday she and her mom went on the stage and testified to what God had told her at camp. Her mother testified how she came home telling her that she is healed and that the doctors will not find the disease in her body anymore because God told her she was healed. Her mother said, "And when they showed up to her appointment to assess her condition, the doctor had to run her test three times and was in complete disbelief. The doctor said, 'There is just no way it can just disappear from your body like this. It is as though you never had it.' Then my daughter looked at her doctor and told him, 'I went to a youth camp, and God told me that I am healed, and I believed Him, so that is why you cannot find it. He healed me because I asked Him to.'"

I am not sure why I had to share this amazing encounter with you. But I really believe it is for you reading this right now. And God is saying to you that you are healed. Please do not doubt Him. He really is not a man that can lie. There is nothing that He cannot do for you, there is nothing He cannot do because absolutely nothing is impossible for Him. There is nothing too small or nothing too vast for Him not to raise up or bring down.

> "God is not a man, that He would lie, Nor a son of man, that He would change His mind; Has He said, and will He not do it? Or has He spoken, and will He not make it good?" (Num. 23:19).

The hand of the Lord was upon me, and He brought me out by the Spirit of the Lord and set me down in the middle of the valley; and it was full of bones. He had me pass among them all around, and behold, there were very many on the surface of the valley; and behold, they were very dry. Then He said to me, "Son of man, can these bones live?" And I answered, "Lord God, You Yourself know." Again, He said to me, "Prophesy over these bones and say to them, 'You dry bones, hear the word of the Lord.' This is what the Lord God says to these bones: 'Behold, I am going to make breath enter you so that you may come to life. And I will attach tendons to you, make flesh grow back on you, cover you with skin, and put breath in you so that you may come to life; and you will know that I am the Lord.'"

> So I prophesied as I was commanded; and as I prophesied, there was a loud noise, and behold, a rattling; and the bones came together, bone to its bone. And I looked, and behold, tendons were on them, and flesh grew and skin covered them; but there was no breath in them. Then He said to me, "Prophesy to the breath, prophesy, son of man, and say to the breath, 'The Lord God says this: "Come from the four winds, breath, and breathe on these slain, so that they come to life."'" So, I prophesied as He commanded me, and the breath entered them, and they came to life and stood on their feet, an exceedingly great army.
>
> —Ezekiel 37:1–10

This same God then is this same God now!

> For as the rain and the snow come down from heaven, And do not return there without watering the earth And making it produce and sprout, And providing seed to the Sower and bread to the eater; So will My word be which goes out of My mouth; It will not return to Me empty, Without accomplishing what I desire, And without succeeding in the purpose for which I sent it.
>
> —Isaiah 55:10–11

God is never far from us; He sees us and knows everything about what we face and what we are about to get ourselves into. Now, as much as you believe that your friends have your back, God does not just have your back but your entire being is in His divine care. Recently a friend of mine who I have known for more than a few years now had cut communications for a while. A few weeks had passed, and I kept hearing this friend's name in my spirit. However, I brushed it aside and continued focusing on what was before me. No matter how often I had brushed off hearing this friends name in my spirit, finally I got annoyed and asked God why was I hearing this friends name in my spirit so often what is going on with them. The Lord then replied to me and said this friend is struggling and their pride is stopping them from calling you. At that moment in my heart my reply was well there is nothing I can do about that.

A week after this conversation with God, the Holy Spirit continuously told me to call this friend, but I just brushing it off or rather slide it aside until I heard that firm daddy's voice which meant business. You know the one where you have your bedroom a hot mess and then your father calls your name from downstairs informing you what time it was for your room. And just by the tone in his voice you knew how serious it was. Well, that is that voice I heard from God and promised Him I would call my friend the next day after work.

In Ecclesiastes 5:4-5 it says when you make a vow or pledge to God, do not put off paying it; for God takes no pleasure in fools who thoughtlessly mock Him. Pay what you vow. It is better that you should not vow than that you should vow and not pay.

Here I was the next day as promised, relaxing on the couch, and just staring beyond the television screen and suddenly I heard God ask me 'did you forget your promise?' I broke from my gaze and picked up my phone and then paused whilst checking the time. When I saw the time, all my fleshly excuses began to surface. Then my thoughts tried to wage war with my spirit saying, 'oh you can make that phone call tomorrow.' While my spirit simply said, 'remember you made a promise to God.'

Opening my contacts on my phone and my flesh still fighting 'you can just call the number and if they do not answer at least you called. After selecting the wrong number and no answer I got puzzled for a few second and asked God well you told me to call so did they change their number? Then as I looked closer realizing it was an older number; I had not deleted it, but I found the new number and called.

As I placed the call to the correct number, my mind could not help but wish for this friend not to pick up the call. However, as the first ringtone began ringing they answered and then I was like bang. Now, we all could agree that I really did not want to make this phone call, however it was not about me. It was about the will of God and who He needed to reach. And this is something we all need to be aware of when we are asking God to use as His vessel.

Yes, I really was reluctant, but I knew there had to be a matter of urgency for God to be so adamant. Upon speaking to this friend, I shared why I was calling and what God had shared with me about them struggling. This left my friend speechless for a couple of minutes and then they began to share all the different struggles mentally, physically, emotionally, and spiritually. Which also caused them to make decisions in the wrong direction. Upon listening to everything I then realized why God had placed this friend constantly in my spirit and God was leading me to open communications so the He could speak through me to them for clarity, guidance, wisdom, and encouragement.

My friend was truly struggling and was drowning, almost losing sight and hope in God. But God was there right by my friend's side and had a plan in motion to get their attention and to prove or rather confirm the direction in which He needed them to go and what to do. I am thankful that the will of God in my life is stronger than my flesh and that God held me to my promise so that His will could be fulfilled .

My friends never try to be a thorn in someone's side or ignore their pain or struggle. Always pay attention to what or who God brings to your spirit and ask questions. When God brings or comes to you urgently, take it seriously and treat it as though your child's life depends on it. Our obedience to the will of God is vital to those whom He has us crossing paths with. If I had not stuck to my promise that evening my friend would have continued to make a permanent decision which would have steered and confused them even further away from His will and direction.

Never try to be a hindrance in someone's life. It is better to be a blessing and a messenger of God's hope and love.

God will never leave us alone in our struggles or confessions. He always has a plan. We just need to acknowledge Him and ask for His directions and follow through.

The Voice of God

Do you remember the first time you heard the voice of God calling you? What was it He said to you? What was it He instructed you to do? Have you done it?

My prayer:

Dear Lord ....

God Knows Your Name

And it came to pass at that time, while Eli was lying down in his place, and when his eyes had begun to grow so dim that he could not see, and before the lamp of God went out in the tabernacle of the Lord where the ark of God was, and while Samuel was lying down, that the Lord called Samuel. And he answered, "Here I am!" So, he ran to Eli and said, "Here I am, for you called me." And he said, "I did not call; lie down again." And he went and lay down. Then the Lord called yet again, "Samuel!" So, Samuel arose and went to Eli, and said, "Here I am, for you called me." He answered, "I did not call, my son; lie down again." Now Samuel did not yet know the Lord, nor was the word of the Lord yet revealed to him. And the Lord called Samuel again the third time. So, he arose and went to Eli, and said, "Here I am, for you did call me." Then Eli perceived that the Lord had called the boy. Therefore, Eli said to Samuel, "Go, lie down; and it shall be, if He calls you, that you must say, 'Speak, Lord, for Your servant hears.'" So Samuel went and lay down in his place. Now the Lord came and stood and called as at other times, "Samuel! Samuel!"

And Samuel answered, "Speak, for Your servant hears."

—1 Samuel 3

Trusting God Today

What are you truly trusting and asking of God to do for you today? You know you have tried it many times your way. I know I did also, but I never really got anywhere in my own strength.

My prayer:

Dear Lord ….

Asking and Seeking

Ask, and it will be given to you; seek, and you will find; knock, and it will be opened to you. For everyone who asks receives, and the one who seeks finds, and to the one who knocks it will be opened. Or what person is there among you who, when his son asks for a loaf of bread, will give him a stone? Or if he asks for a fish, he will not give him a snake, will he? So, if you, despite being evil, know how to give good gifts to your children, how much more will your Father who is in heaven give good things to those who ask Him!

—Matthew 7:7–11

Believe or Doubt—You Choose

"Faith and fear cannot dwell in the same flowers pot."

What is it that you are believing but doubting at the same time in God for?

Doubt and faith cannot dwell in the same temple. In other words, your mind cannot be doubting while your heart is trying to trust faithfully. This will surely create an unstable storm within, like a raging sea.

My prayer:

Dear Lord ….

Prayer for Wisdom

Now if any of you lacks wisdom, let him ask God, who gives to all generously and without reproach; and it will be given to him. But let him ask in trust, doubting nothing; for the doubter is like a wave in the sea being tossed and driven by the wind. Indeed, that person should not think that he will receive anything from the Lord, because he is double-minded, unstable in all his ways.

—James 1:5–8

Prayer
Heavenly Father…

My Prayer for You

My friend, I pray for whatever it is you are believing from God. I pray that you believe in Him with your faith, that it breaks down every stronghold off you, your entire household, and your children's children in the mighty name of Yeshua Hamashiach [Jesus Christ]. Amen.

Just believe. It takes a lot more not to believe than it does to. You have much more to gain than to lose in believing.

Every Mountain High, Every Valley Low

"He who dwells in the secret place of El Elyon (God Most High) shall abide under the shadow of El Shaddai (God Almighty). I will say of Yahuah, He is my refuge and fortress: my Elohim (the creator of heavens and the earth) in him will I trust" (Ps. 91:1–2, Cepher).

The word of the Lord came to Jonah the son of Amittai, saying, "Arise, go to Nineveh, the great city, and cry out against it, because their wickedness has come up before Me." But Jonah got up to flee to Tarshish from the presence of the Lord. So he went down to Joppa, found a ship that was going to Tarshish, paid the fare, and boarded it to go with them to Tarshish away from the presence of the Lord.
However, the Lord hurled a great wind on the sea and there was a great storm on the sea, so that the ship was about to break up. Then the sailors became afraid, and every man cried out to his god, and they hurled the cargo which was in the ship into the sea to lighten it for them. But Jonah had gone below into the stern of the

ship, had lain down, and fallen sound asleep. So, the captain approached him and said, "How is it that you are sleeping? Get up, call on your god! Perhaps your god will be concerned about us so that we will not perish." And each man said to his mate, "Come, let's cast lots so that we may find out on whose account this catastrophe has struck us." So, they cast lots, and the lot fell on Jonah. Then they said to him, "tell us, now! On whose account has this catastrophe struck us? What is your occupation, and where do you come from? What is your country, and from what people are you?" So, he said to them, "I am a Hebrew, and I fear the Lord God of heaven who made the sea and the dry land."

Then the men became extremely afraid, and they said to him, "How could you do this?" For the men knew that he was fleeing from the presence of the Lord, because he had told them. So, they said to him, "What should we do to you so that the sea will become calm for us?"—for the sea was becoming increasingly stormy. And he said to them, "Pick me up and hurl me into the sea. Then the sea will become calm for you because I know that on account of me this great storm has come upon you." However, the men rowed desperately to return to land, but they could not, because the sea was becoming even stormier against them. Then they cried out to the Lord and said, "We earnestly pray, O Lord, do not let us perish on account of this man's life, and do not put innocent blood on us; for You, Lord, have done as You pleased."

So, they picked up Jonah and hurled him into the sea, and the sea stopped its raging. Then the men became extremely afraid of the Lord, and they offered a sacrifice to the Lord and made vows. And the Lord designated a great fish to swallow Jonah, and Jonah was in the stomach of the fish for three days and three nights.

Then Jonah prayed to the Lord his God from the stomach of the fish, and he said, "I called out of my distress to the Lord, And He answered me. I called for help from the depth of Sheol; You heard my voice. For You threw me into the deep, Into the heart of the seas, And the current flowed around me. All Your breakers and waves passed over me. So, I said, 'I have been cast out of Your sight.

Nevertheless, I will look again toward Your holy temple.' Water encompassed me to the point of death. The deep flowed around me, Seaweed was wrapped around my head. I descended to the base of the mountains. The earth with its bars was around me forever, But You have brought up my life from the pit, Lord my God. While I was fainting away, I remembered the Lord.

And my prayer came to You, Into Your holy temple. Those who are followers of worthless idols Abandon their faithfulness, but I will sacrifice to You With a voice of thanksgiving. That which I have vowed I will pay. Salvation is from the Lord." Then the Lord commanded the fish, and it vomited Jonah up onto the dry land.

Now the word of the Lord came to Jonah the second time, saying, "Arise, go to Nineveh, the great city, and proclaim to it the proclamation which I am going to tell you." So Jonah got up and went to Nineveh according to the word of the Lord. Now Nineveh was an exceedingly large city, a three days' walk. Then Jonah began to go through the city one day's walk; and he cried out and said, "Forty more days, and Nineveh will be overthrown."

Then the people of Nineveh believed in God; and they called a fast and put on sackcloth, from the greatest to the least of them. When the word reached the king of Nineveh, he got up from his throne, removed his robe from himself, covered himself with sackcloth, and sat on the dust. And he issued a proclamation, and it said, "In Nineveh by the decree of the king and his nobles: No person, animal, herd, or flock is to taste anything. They are not to eat, or drink water. But every person and animal must be covered with sackcloth; and people are to call on God vehemently, and they are to turn, each one from his evil way, and from the violence which is in their hands. Who knows, God may turn and relent, and turn from His burning anger so that we will not perish." When God saw their deeds, that they turned from their evil way, then God relented of the disaster which He had declared He would bring on them. So, He did not do it.

But it greatly displeased Jonah, and he became angry. Then he prayed to the Lord and said, "Please Lord, was this not what I said when I was still in my own country? Therefore, in anticipation of this I fled to Tarshish, since I knew that You are a gracious and compassionate God, slow to anger and abundant in mercy, and One who relents of disaster. So now, Lord, please take my life from me, for death is better to me than life." But the Lord said, "Do you have a good reason to be angry?"

Then Jonah left the city and sat down east of it. There he made a shelter for himself and sat under it in the shade, until he could see what would happen in the city. So, the Lord God designated a plant, and it grew up over Jonah to be a shade over his head, to relieve him of his discomfort. And Jonah was overjoyed about the plant. But God designated a worm when dawn came the next day, and it attacked the plant and it withered. And when the sun came up God designated a scorching east wind, and the sun beat down on Jonah's head so that he became faint, and he begged with all his soul to die, saying, "Death is better to me than life!"

But God said to Jonah, "Do you have a good reason to be angry about the plant?" And he said, "I have good reason to be angry, even to the point of death!" Then the Lord said, "You had compassion on the plant, for which you did not work and which you did not cause to grow, which came up overnight and perished overnight. Should I not also have compassion on Nineveh, the great city in which there are more than 120,000 people, who do not know the difference between their right hand and their left, as well as many animals?"

—Jonah 1–4

Why did I begin with the entire book of Jonah, you may be asking yourselves? Well, firstly, not many of us (me included) have sat down and read its entirety. We only know the basics of the story or the song from Sunday school. What if I inform you that we have all had a Jonah moment of disobedience along our journey with God. We have done it repeatedly. There are times we are not recognizing that we are being disobedient until lightning flash and the thunder roar.

We may not have been swallowed by a massive fish like Jonah trying to flee from the Presence of God. However, in some aspect, it seems as when God pulls 360 degrees on us to turn around like the massive fish being directed by God to take Jonah to the city of Nineveh. And secondly because the Spirit of God brought it to my attention and showed me how it is related to this very journey beyond a journey.

Just get to the water, come on you can do this! Just hold on, hold it together. He leads you be the still waters; He restores you soul." I kept encouraging myself. "Lord, I cannot breathe, I just cannot go any further. I am just one person, just one! How do you expect me to go any further without any help? Humbly I came, You asked me to trust you. Everything You have asked me to do amid opposition after opposition. They call me names, they look down on me, they mock me and yet You have me standing during it all.

I cry out to the Lord with my voice; With my voice to the Lord I make my supplication. I pour out my complaint before Him; I declare before Him my trouble. When my spirit was overwhelmed within me, Then You knew my path. In the way in which I walk They have secretly set a snare for me. Look on my right hand and see, For there is no one who acknowledges me; Refuge has failed me; No one cares for my soul. I cried out to You, O Lord:

I said, "You are my refuge, My portion in the land of the living. Attend to my cry, For I am brought very low; Deliver me from my persecutors, For they are stronger than I. Bring my soul out of prison, That I may praise Your name; The righteous shall surround me, For You shall deal bountifully with me."

—Psalm 142

> Blessed are you when people insult you and persecute you, and falsely say all kinds of evil against you because of Me. Rejoice and be glad, for your reward in heaven is great; for in this same way, they persecuted the prophets who were before you.
>
> —Matthew 5:11-12

Father, You told me to give it all up, just to trust You, and to have faith. How much more faith must I have? You have me pouring out my heart, and this is what my reward is? Hurt? How long have You had me standing and believing that this will all be for Your glory? Is this what You wanted it to be like? Was this all along the ending which You had in store for me? If you knew this was how the story goes, why did You call me in the first place, and why did you have me go through those valleys, climbing those mountains, just to reach this point of betrayal and brokenness?

Why does everything have to be a fight just for a breakthrough with You? This entire journey You have stripped me naked. You peeled away all my defenses, and for what purpose? I did not call myself, You called me and promised to be with me. How can people treat others like this in Your "house"? What manner of "house" is this? Are You even in this "house"?

What breed of vipers are these that show one face of venom and the other sweet as honey? Lord, I am weak; there is no more fight left within me. It is a constant battle over and over. Sitting in silence, I am wounded more, serving without being seen by many, I am wounded more and standing in the midst, worshipping, I am wounded and broken even more. Yet still You whisper in my heart to just close my eyes and raise my hands up toward heaven and worship You.

> The eyes of the Lord are toward the righteous, And His ears are toward their cry for help.

> The face of the Lord is against evildoers, to eliminate the memory of them from the earth. The righteous cry out, and the Lord hears and rescues them from all their troubles. The Lord is near to the brokenhearted and saves those who are crushed in spirit.
>
> —Psalm 34:15–18

I am out of tears, Father. Please do not allow my tears to touch the ground. There is no more room left on my chest to receive any more blows. And this last blow is above and beyond any other blows I was able to withstand. This one rocked me to my very core. Have I been a muppet, and now I am having all these flashbacks? Where You have carried me from, how You proved Yourself repeatedly? So, what is this before me, and how does any of this make any sense to me, Lord. Wait, there is no way I would have called myself to such an assignment. Have I been naïve to believe Your words are to be trusted, God? Do You still expect me to love unconditionally? Is this why it hurts even deeper? How do You still expect me to remain standing after witnessingthis?

> The afflictions of the righteous are many, But the Lord rescues him from them all. He protects all his bones, not one of them is broken. The Lord redeems the souls of His servants,
> And none of those who take refuge in Him will suffer for their guilt.
>
> —Psalm 34:19–22

Whatever we do in secret and behind closed doors or anywhere else, the light of God will always shine bright and bring it all to the surface. A small lie is still a lie, and a slight lie is still a lie, just as partial disobedience is still disobedience in its entirety. If you believe that your own dishonesty, slack behavior, rebellious spirit, and disobedience will only affect you alone, you are sadly mistaken because it indeed causes a ripple effect with the lives that are assigned to you by God.

Our obedience to God carries a lot of responsibilities, yes, and it may not be an easy assignment. However, when we lean on our own understanding, this is where we find ourselves trying to serve two different masters. We then find ourselves thinking we can juggle the manner of Heaven and the crystals together. These two can never be compared because one represents the provision of God, while the other plays tricks and present itself as a fake platter. Not all platters are good for us to eat from. Some of those platters create distractions and feed off our emotions, driving us further and further away from those God has called us to.

Our actions of disobedience in the will of God always cause a chain of reactions to those around us, near or far, physically and spiritually.

It is about to be my stop; this ride feels much longer than it should. Finally, I dump my bag on the bed, kick off my heels, and put on my flats. Grabbing only my keys and phone, I flew out the front door again. It only took me less than five minutes to get to the ocean. As my feet touched the boardwalk and the ocean breeze hit my face, the tears came flooding down uncontrollably. It was not a stormy afternoon, but the waves sure were acting as though it was.

As I sat on the edge of the rocks and as crowded as the beach was, the only sound I could hear was the waves crashing violently along the rocks. The more the waves crashed, the heavier the tears fell as though the weight of the tears could no longer be stored deep within. I yelled, "God, has all of this been a waste of Your time and my time? Have my tears been in vain and fell to the ground without any harvest? You called me, and I answered even though it was against all human logic. Yet here I am again pouring out my heart to You. I am just one person alone. How much more will You allow me to go through without Your help? You said You would never give us more than what we could handle. Well, this feels a lot more than that. Just a little help, that is all

I am asking, for a little help. Is that too much to ask for? You took me away from everything and everyone I have ever known to follow You. Your will for my life and many did not understoodd it nor do they have to. I understand that, but just a little help, is there no break between these constant blows? Is there no peace during any of this? Does it all have to be such a fight just to get a pinch of breakthrough? Why does this feel like that first crossroad where I was with You?"

> By faith Abraham, when he was called, obeyed by going out to a place which he was to receive for an inheritance; and he left, not knowing where he was going. By faith he lived as a stranger in the land of promise, as in a foreign land, living in tents with Isaac and Jacob, fellow heirs of the same promise; for he was looking for the city which has foundations, whose architect and builder is God.
>
> —Hebrews 11:8–10

"You know my heart, Lord. You must see how I am feeling, and You should know my thoughts. You cannot expect me to remain in such a place where my wounds are forever getting deeper and deeper. And there is no sign of hope or relief to breathe and catch my breath. Lord, I am tired, I am tired of it all. Anything else but this, do not ask me to return because clearly You have me on this side trusting and walking in obedience, but on the other hand is an entirely different story. Did I miss the memo? Am I losing my marbles or what? Lord, I am done talking. That is it, just because You have been shining on my meekness this does not make me clueless."

When I lift my eyes to the hills, where does my help come from? Heavenly father, my only help comes from You. You are the maker of heaven and earth. Father, I know You will not allow my feet to be moved because You oh Lord are my anchor. Lord, You are the one who keeps me safe and secure. You do not slumber, nor do You sleep. Father, You are the only one who keeps Israel. Lord, You are my keeper forever, You are the glory and the lifter of my head. Heavenly father, You are my shade at my right hand. And the sun will not strike me during the day nor will the moon during the night. For You oh Lord, have and will continue to preserve me from all evil and evildoers. My soul, You will preserve oh my God, You alone will preserve my feet as I go out and as I enter back in from now on and forevermore.

—Psalm 121

As I sat there on the edge of the rocks, I had nothing else to say to God, maybe because I was finished with the journey He had called me to, or maybe because my entire being was just numb. I could still hear the ocean; however, the waves were calmer and smoother. I looked around, and to my surprise, there were still a few people walking by behind me. And for some strange reason it felt as though time had stood still and no one was around me as I poured out to God.

"In my distress I cried to the Lord, And He heard me. Deliver my soul, O Lord, from lying lips and from a deceitful tongue" (Ps. 120:1–2).

The tears began to stop, and I was looking out on the water with no thoughts within my being, just blankness. Suddenly, I heard my phone began to play a song of worship. The song that began to play seemed to have a message in it, but I skipped it and another and another. Then the message in the song hit me, and I thought, "Wait, are You trying to say something to me, Lord?" And then I heard God whispered to me, "I need you to believe, I need you to believe as though an unbeliever's life depends on it. Do not lose your hope in Me. It is your anchor in Me which keeps you."

"Believe as though an unbeliever's life depends on it? And do not lose my hope in You?" I repeated to myself, how do I even begin to do that with how I am feeling? Wait, where has all the heaviness gone? Father, did You take it all from me? Why do I still have this unconditional love within, ever deeper, as reverence to you in obedience?

A Prayer Inspired by Psalm 77

I cried out to You, oh God, with my voice. To You, Father, I cried out, and You attend Your ears to my cry. In my time of distress, I sought You, Almighty God. My hands are stretched out to You day and night without ceasing. Heavenly Father, my soul refused to be comforted by anyone else except You. When I remember God and all the mountains and valleys of this journey, I feel troubled all over again. When I complain, it just causes my spirit to be overwhelmed. As tired as I feel, You hold my eyelids open, and my heart is so troubled that I cannot speak when I look up toward heaven and consider the days of old and the years of ancient times.

I am called to remember my song in the night, which I meditate within my heart. My spirit is searching diligently for You. Father, come and walk with me. Lord, speak to my heart because You alone know its true rhythm. Lord, will You cast me off from Your presence forever? Is this Your way of testing my trust in You? Shall I never find favor in Your sight or has Your mercy ceased from me forever? Have Your promises to me fail and have fallen to the ground, or did You change Your mind toward me? Are You angry with me that You have forgotten to be gracious toward me and not close Your tender mercies toward me? Is this all the anguish I must endure just for picking up my cross to follow You? But as I sit here, I am remembering all the years of Your gracious right hand, oh God. How you molded me, breathed life back into my dry bones, of how You lifted me up and set my feet on solid

A Prayer Inspired by Psalm 77

ground. I am remembering Your mighty works, Father. Your wonders of old I do remember, parting the Red Sea, closing the mouths of lions, and opening prison doors.

I will remember Your years of old and meditate on all Your works. My heart and lips will declare all Your deeds. I will not withhold my testimony of how great You are and of how great You continue to be with me. Your ways, oh God, are in the secret places of Your Presence. There is no other god who could ever measure up to You, for You are the great King and Lord of all things, great and small. You are the God who does wonders and You, oh God, have declared Your mighty strength over us all. With Your arms, You have redeemed Your children. The waters saw You, oh God, the waters see You and were afraid. Help me to continue walking in reverence of You and Your mighty Presence. As the depth trembles, the cloud pours out water, and the skies sent out a sound, Father, I ask You to take me to deeper depths in Your Word and Presence. Open the floodgates of Heaven, and pour out a fresh anointing over me. Lord, I see Your arrows flash about me, and I hear the voice of Your thunder in the whirlwind. Your lightning lit up our world. Even the earth trembles and shakes. Your ways were always in the sea and Your path in the great waters. Your footsteps not yet known to us, but You led us Your people like a flock by the hand of Your servants Moses and Aaron. I thank You for such grace and compassion.

As the sun began to set in the distance, I arose and went closer to the water. Dipping my feet in the ocean, I told myself that every day this week I would stop by here. The days passed by, and I have caught almost all of the sunrise on the beach. My mind has been so focused on work and wanting just to be by the water so much so that all my thoughts from Sunday were like a distant memory.

However, on my way back home, sitting on the bus and looking out the window, I thought I could use this time to check all my messages. After all, I ignored them all for five days now. As I scanned through with my eyes on the usual names, I saw a name that was not so usual after all. "Oh, my goodness," I said to myself, "I have not heard from her in such a long time. Wow, maybe a year or more." Even though her name was not the first in the messages, I went straight to hers and opened the message. Upon finishing reading her message, immediately I responded and informed her that I was off work on Saturday. So whatever time is good for her will be great for me to catch up on the telephone.

Feeling happy, I was looking forward to catching up with my dear friend and sister in Christ. As I headed out to catch the Saturday morning sunrise, all I could imagine was just the peace and quiet and the touch of the sand on my feet. I entered the beach, and it was beautiful. There were one or two people in the distance, walking.

Sitting not too far from the lifeguard's hut, I sat in the sand and breathed out, closing my eyes as I breathed in and out. "Oh, how my heart longs for you, Lord. I surrender it all to You. Take all of it, and just give me Your peace," I said to God, as I looked out toward the sun rising with such radiance, grace, and beauty. It was then my spirit reminded me of Psalm 23, and I began to pray it:

> Father, You alone are my north, east, south, and west. You are the only compass I know to follow. You have never left me to lack, even when I fail to see Your light at the end of my tunnels. No matter where You call me to, Father, You provided for my head to lay in comfort in green pastures. Though I face many dismays that try to overwhelm me, You continue to lead me here by Your still waters. Not only to refresh, but also to restore my spirit and soul within me. When I try to pave my own paths with my own understanding, You never fail to lead me right back to Your path of righteousness and peace. All for Your name's sake, and to You belong all the glory. When I must face trials and tribulations and am surrounded by all forms of uncertain darkness, which causes my heart to fear, You never fail to comfort and remind me to never fear because You are forever with

A Prayer Inspired by Psalm 77

me, and Your comfort and console gives me rest. When I am surrounded by all adversaries who have chosen to revolt against me, only You alone knows why. But still, You are faithful to prepare a table of grace before me in the very presences of all my adversaries. Father, You continue to shower me with love and strength. You alone anoint my head with Your everlasting oil, pouring out knowledge, wisdom, and understanding of things beyond anything I could ever fathom. Lord, surely Your goodness and mercy will always be with me all the days of my life. As I seek to always dwell in Your presence and house, always. Amen. (See Psalm 77.)

I stayed in that spot for a couple of hours, and before heading back home I just had to take a dip in the water from head to toes. It was not until later in the late part of the evening, just before sunset that my friend and I began talking over the telephone. After going back and forth about how we, each were, she began to share her dream, which I was in, with God giving her a word of encouragement for me.

Please believe me when I tell you that when our Heavenly Father needs to get your attention, He will always do it in such a way that you yourself cannot deny it is Him. Now yet again, this is the same friend whom God had used to get my attention a couple years prior with my three questions. So, I believe this vessel was more than trustworthy, whom God has chosen again.

Now, when my friend called me, I was making my way back from running errands. Just before I got off at my stop, my phone rang, and it sure was wonderful to hear her voice. It was like we just continued off from where we last spoke, as though the physical distance between us never existed. Anyhow, as she began to give me details of her dream, at first, I was speechless, and then I said to her, "No wait, stop. Give me two minutes to drop these bags down indoor, and then I call you back on video, and I will show you my location live."

In her dream, God showed my dear friend where I was walking and crying, making my way to the boardwalk and the rock upon which I sat, and most of all seeing me sitting there crying and asking God for help. Her details were so clear and precise as if she had been in my location before. And she had never been to that state or city before.

Without unpacking the bags, I grabbed my backup charger because I knew this was going to be a few hours kind of conversation. As I walked out the front door again, I video called her back, adjusting the camera outwards so she could see where I was and the path, I always take to the boardwalk but especially that Sunday when I was crying.

Before I began to say much about the path, she began to confirm with me that it was exactly what God had shown her. As I entered the boardwalk, it was also exactly as in her dream and the rock which I sat on. As she continued to talk, I found myself zoning out, hearing only the waves crashing along the shore. My mind was asking so many questions of how this could really be possible for her to know this area and yet she had never been here before.

My heart felt overwhelmed with awe, wonder, and tears. Tears because I was realizing that God had been listening to me. But not only was He listening, He was sitting with me. He had never left me, and He was never far from me. Most of all, He already had a plan, a plan to confirm that He is with me. Oh my God, how great are Your thoughts toward me, for I truly am in the palm of Your Mighty hands.

As my friend continued reminding me of His words and encouraging me, I began to cry. This cry was not out of sadness but from a grateful and humble heart. A cry of realizing that even though I might be surrounded by adversaries, He still called me out by name, and greater is He who is in me than those who have set up camp around me.

"Ayoka, remember who you are and whose you are? Do not go allowing anyone to put out your light. He says to tell you do not let go of His hands. Do not let go of your hope in Him. And no matter where He has led you to, He had a plan. He does not change His mind, so keep your focus on Him and keep trusting Him all the way," she finished off saying before we ended our video call. We had been on the call for over four hours. I am not sure what kind of help I was looking for from God. However, this was not the type of help I was expecting, but on the other hand, God knew the type of help I needed and not wanted so that when all was said and done, all the glory would go right back to Him.

See Yourself in the Word of God

I love You, O Lord, my strength. You are my Lord, my rock, my fortress, and my deliverer. My God, my strength, in whom I will and have trusted in. Father, You are my shield and the horn of my salvation and my stronghold. I will call upon You, Lord, who is worthy to be praised; so, shall I be saved from my enemies. You have sent from above and took me; Father, You drew me out of many waters and delivered me from my strong enemy, from those who hated me, for they were too strong for me. They confronted me in the day of my calamity, but You, almighty God, were my support. You also brought me out into a broad place and delivered me because You delighted in me, for You will light my lamp.

My Lord and my God, enlighten my darkness. For by You, God, I can run against a troop and can leap over a wall. Lord, your way is perfect, and all Your words are proven. Father, You are a shield to all who take refuge and trust in You. For who is God, except the Lord? And who is a rock, except You, almighty God? It is You, oh Lord, who arms me with strength and makes my way perfect. Father, it is You who makes my feet like the feet of deer and sets me on my high places. You have also given me the shield of Your salvation; Your right hand has held me up, Your gentleness has made me great. You enlarged my path under me so my feet did not slip. For You have armed me with strength for the battle; You have subdued under me those who revolted against me. The Lord lives! Blessed be my Rock! Let the God of my salvation be exalted. It is God who avenges me and subdues the peoples under me; He delivers me from my enemies. You also lift me up above those who rise against me; You have delivered me from the violent man. (See Psalm 18.)

Moments along Your Journey

You know there are moments along our journey where we will feel weak, tired, frustrated, overwhelmed, and just lost amid the people around us. Often, we try to fill these areas of frustrations with meaningless distractions, and yet we meet the same walls of questions. What is my purpose of being here? Why am I here? What difference am I making? What is my worth, my value? Why can't I just have it all together like everyone else? Is it okay to ask myself these questions?

Personally, I used to think to myself, "snap out of it. Why are you doubting? Get yourself together. Don't you already know who God is? Don't you know that a man who is double minded is unstable in all his ways, and God does not love an unstable man? Don't you know that you are a chosen people, a royal priesthood, a Holy nation, and God's special possession?" (1 Pet. 2:9). I believe no matter who you are and where you may be in your journey of faith, you will get to this stage or rather this valley of questions. However, it is important, because you find yourself in the secret place of the Most High God. Or you try to fill the void with worldly knowledge causing you to be more spiritually dead and blind.

It was not that I doubted God; it was more of wanting it "now" instead of wanting to wait and learn more, grow more, physically and spiritually. Maybe if I have it now, all the questions I have will just disappear. But this is not so; we cannot just jump over the bridge to get to the other side. To know if the bridge can withstand the weight we carry, we will have to walk across it or drive across it. How do you know to trust God if you do not allow Him to lead? Not to lead part way and then you take over because you think you know best.

Recently I was visiting a dear sister in Christ. We spent the day going through a few nature trails. Funny enough, all the tiny little things I was reserved on and was fearful of, I saw not one. Anyhow, after we got back to the house for lunch and took a break, we went out again, but this time on the golf cart. I mean, who does not like a nice stroll on a golf cart around their neighborhood. There were a few hills and valleys but nothing that would scare you out of your own shadow, or that was what I thought.

After heading back on the golf cart, we ventured out a different route, steeper hills to go up and crooked paths that would make you think, "Oh, heck no, this golf cart cannot handle such," and you would want to turn around to go back the normal route. Could you imagine I trusted this golf cart to drive around until I saw the real hills and valleys and then had doubt that it would not be able to handle such challenges? Is this not like our walk and faith in God along our journeys?

Before we got closer to the crooked turns, I was all excited and thought, "Oh yes, let's raise our hands in the air as though we were on a rollercoaster ride." However, when I saw my friend raise her hands, I yelled, "No, no, no, not you, you keep your hands on that wheel" as she laughed at me. We started to turn on the crooked hill, and my heart began beating overwhelmingly fast. What seemed fun was not looking like fun, and my entire trust in the golf cart came to a complete end with screams and fear. I wanted to get off and trust what I knew best even if it would take me a little longer, oh yes, my own two legs.

My only thought was, "I need to get off this thing, just stop and let me walk." But she insisted we would be fine. "It's okay," she said while laughing her face off at me. I almost wet myself screaming; however, we laughed the entire way home. As we approached the driveway, which by the way was downhill, that was the fastest I jumped off as she slowed down.

Now, was there anything wrong with the golf cart? The answer is no, there was nothing wrong with it. It was fully working and able to drive on all surfaces and was built to drive in difficult conditions. However, it was my perception of what was in front of me. And instead of trusting the driver and believing that the cart was more than able to endure, I allowed what I saw around me to affect my heart and faith.

> After He had dismissed the crowds, He went up on the mountain by Himself to pray. When it was evening, He was there alone. But the boat by this time was already a long distance from land, tossed and battered by the waves; for the wind was against them. And in the fourth watch of the night (3:00–6:00 a.m.) Jesus came to them, walking on the sea. When the disciples saw Him walking on the sea, they were terrified, and said, "It is a ghost!" And they cried out in fear. But immediately He spoke to them, saying, "Take courage, it is I! Do not be afraid!" Peter replied to Him, "Lord, if it is really You, command me to come to You on the water." He said, "Come!" So, Peter got out of the boat, and walked on the water and came toward Jesus. But when he saw the effects of the wind, he was frightened, and he began to sink, and he cried out, "Lord, save me!" Immediately Jesus extended His hand and caught him, saying to him, "O you of little faith, why did you doubt?"

This is a lesson for us all with our everyday journey in God, our Heavenly Father. Though we say and somewhat pretend to trust Him, when it comes to those crooked corners in our lives, we allow doubt and fear to take over because our eyes are no longer on him but on the distractions, which in the end drift us so far out in the deep end, causing us to lose sight of who we are in Him, what He has called us to, and most importantly, who He is in us.

If we are not feeding on the Word of God daily, drawing close to Him, praying and seeking Him in all that we do, we too will become weary and drained as the world, while walking around like a headless chicken and not knowing where we belong or who we serve.

If we do not read the Word of God, we will never know what to do or know how to encourage ourselves. Nor will we know how to keep renewing our minds daily in His Presence. The Word of God is true, and it is sharper than any two-edged sword. It gives us life, it gives us knowledge, wisdom, and understanding. Read it for yourself, do not just be hearers of it. Do not allow yourselves to be complacent by just hearing of it or hear someone else reading it. We all have the authority to read His divine Word for ourselves. No one else will be held accountable for the same knowledge that you had the same access to and did not make time to read and seek our Heavenly Father's counsel for yourself. Yes, faith does come by hearing and hearing the Word. We cannot just be hearers of the word and not doers also.

> Therefore, ridding yourselves of all filthiness and all that remains of wickedness, in humility receive the word implanted, which can save your souls. But prove yourselves doers of the word, and not just hearers who deceive themselves. For if anyone is a hearer of the word and not a doer, he is like a man who looks at his natural face in a mirror; for once he has looked at himself and gone away, he has immediately forgotten what kind of person he was. But one who has looked intently at the perfect law, the law of freedom, and has continued in it, not having become a forgetful hearer but an active doer, this person will be blessed in what he does.
>
> —James 1:21–25

A Prayer of Inspiration from Psalm 27

Oh, Heavenly Father, You are my light and salvation; because of You, I do not have to fear. You are the stronghold of my life, Who gives me the confidence to remain standing when the wicked tries to come against me, to overwhelm and destroy my heart and spirit. Oh my Lord, You cause all those who have arisen against me to stumble and fall. Father, even though an army of adversaries encamp against me, my heart will not fear, and in this I am confident and will keep trusting You. My Lord, my Savior and risen King, one thing I have always desired of You: that I will seek all the days of my life, that I may live in Your house, Your Presence, Your light, and under the shadow of Your mighty wings all the days of my life. And to seek the beauty of Your Holiness. Heavenly Father, in the days of trouble conceal me in Your tabernacle. Almighty God, You will hide me in the secret place of Your pavilion and will set me high on a rock.

In this, my head shall now be lifted up above my enemies all around me; therefore, I will offer up sacrifices of joy in Your house, I will sing, oh yes, I will sing praises to You, oh Lord. My Savior and King, hear me when I cry with my voice to You. Oh, have mercy upon me and answer me. When You said, "Seek My face," my heart, oh Lord, said to You, "Your face, Lord, I will seek." Father, please do not hide Your face from me, do not turn Your servant away in anger. For You have been my only help and have never left me. Father, do not leave nor forsake me now, oh God, of my salvation. For when my mother and my father forsake me, then You, oh Lord, will take great care of me.

Heavenly Father, teach me Your ways, oh God, and lead me in a smooth path, because of my enemies. Almighty God, do not deliver me into the will of any of my adversaries. For they give false witnesses with my name and have revolted against me. And such have also breathed out violence against me. Father, I would have lost heart if I had not believed that I would have seen Your Goodness, oh Lord, in the land of the living.

Oh Lord, You alone know all things, and though I may struggle at times, in the stillness of Your love my heart shall wait on You, Lord, and be of good courage with worship in my heart to You. I know that You, oh Lord, shall strengthen my heart, and I will wait, I will wait on You, Father. (See Psalm 27.)

There is a huge difference between wanting to do things our way and allowing and following God's way. At the end of the day, He knows all things, great and small. He knows the deepest darkest thoughts, our fears, our what-ifs, our maybes, our yes and our no. As we are reminded in Jeremiah 29:11, "For I know what plans I have in mind for you,' says The Lord of Host 'plans for well-being, not for bad things; so that you can have hope and a future."

We constantly make our own plans and are truly deceived by thinking that we oversee our own destiny, ability, and our own blueprint. But we must remember the moment we gave our lives to Yeshua Hamashiach (the Son of God) we became one with Him and the Father. We confess that He is Lord and Savior of our lives, and we repent daily and ask for forgiveness of our sins, which we receive freely, not working for it or even deserving it, but only because He loves us and calls us friends—friends who are joint heir of the Kingdom of the Most High God, our Elohim, our El Shaddai, our Prince of peace.

My friends seek God's wisdom while it is soughtable, knock on heaven's gate while it is visible. Because there will come a time when neither of these shall be possible. That whisper that we often hear, "Oh, you have time," let me remind you time waits for no man and no woman, no one. And a lot of us have fallen for this repeatedly. The enemy does not just come to steel, kill, and destroy. He starts off with lies and distractions. The time we spend on nonsense here, there, and everywhere, in the blink of an eye we find ourselves wondering on the what-ifs, buts, and maybes. Living a life of regrets is not living at all, and then you find yourself living a life of cycles. And all the time that has then passed by can never be given back to you. Get it right now so you will never have to look back and wonder or regret the opportunities and the many doors and lives God could have and would have used you to change but most of all be a blessing to.

Do the right thing now, follow the Lord's calling on your life now; make a change now, step out with courage and faith in Him now, trust Him now, try Him now, pray now, move now, have faith now, stand now. Your season is now—do not delay anymore.

Lift Up Your Head

Oh, lift your heads, you daughters and sons of Zion give thanks to the Most High, our El Shaddai, with all your hearts. Testify of all His marvelous wonders. Be happy and celebrate in Him, sing songs of praises to the Most High, the creator of Heaven and Earth. The Earth is the Lord's and all its fullness, the world, and those who live in it. Lift up your heads, you daughters and sons of the Most High, and be lifted up, you ancient doors so that Our King of glory may come in. Who is the King of glory, they ask. The Lord Strong and Mighty, the Lord Might in battle. The God of Hosts, He is the glorious King.

Abba, You have searched me deeply and know me. You know my every move when I am sitting and when I am standing. Abba, You understand all my thoughts from far away, You examine my every path and all my lying downs. My ways You are more acquainted with than I could ever comprehend. Even before a word appear on my tongue, Father, You know it all. Abba, you are ever before me and behind me, protecting and guiding my every steps. Your mighty hands are ever upon me for comfort, and it is like none other. Abba Your touch on my life is beyond anything I could ever comprehend; it is life, and it is love like none other.

But where could I ever hide from Your Spirit, Father, or even run from Your peaceful Presence? If I ascend to the Heavens, Abba, You are there awaiting me, and if I try to make my own path, You Abba are also there calling me back to Your heart of truth and worship. When I tried to take the wings of dawn and travel to the remotest part of the country, to my astonishment even there, Abba, You never left me and caused Your hands to lead me, while Your right hand took a hold of me. Surely, I was surrounded by darkness, but will it forever overwhelm me?

As the sun and moon shines light at different stages, they are one and the same to You, Abba. You crafted my innermost parts with such delight and love as You wove me in Your daughter's womb. I am forever humbled and thankful to You, Abba. Because You have created me with such grace, such meekness, such love and enduring strength and humility, with much more than I could ever imagine. Your work, Abba, is forever wonderful and glorious, and this my soul knows all too well. Father, as I was being made in secret, no part of my frame was hidden from You. Abba, Your eyes saw my formless substance, and in Your book were written all the days which You have ordained for me, when yet there was not one of them. Abba, how precious are all Your thoughts over me. Oh, how vast is the sum of them all; if I tried to count them, they would outnumber all the grains of sand. Whenever I am awake, You are always with me as I am with You.

Abba, I desire for You to search me always and know all that is within my heart forever. Put me through the fire and test me, and if You find any thoughts which are not of You, please replace them all with Your wisdom, knowledge, and peace. Your peace surpasses all comprehension. Create in me a river flowing with Your grace and compassion for those I am blessed to cross path with. Shine Your light of grace within me, and if there are any seeds or any infested roots of unforgiveness in me, Father, I surrender it all to Your will and ask you to uproot it all and heal the wounds of my heart. Enlarge my heart to love like You do, Lord, enlarge my heart to see and love unconditionally as You, and forever lead me in Your way everlasting. Amen.

He Has a Plan

"For I know the plans and thoughts that I have for you, says the Lord, plans for peace and well-being and not for disaster, to give you a future and a hope" (Jer. 29:11).

A Journey of Surrendering and Back into the Father's Arms of Grace

◇◇

> For the weapon of our warfare are not of the flesh, but divinely powerful for the destruction of fortresses. We are destroying speculations and every lofty things raised up against the knowledge of God, and we are taking every thought captive to the obedience of Yeshua Hamashiach.
>
> —2 Corinthians 10:4–5

So was it worth it? I bet it was not. It may have sounded great when you first came up with the idea, right? And now it has been the worst decision you have ever made in your life. Oh, wait—everyone was cheering you on and whispering how amazing it would be. And naturally, you went along with it because you were feeling all the fake positive vibes.

Now how do you feel? Where are all those fake positive vibes that were cheering you on? Do you not find it strange how we often try to fight with God? With the matters pertaining deep within our hearts and those around us not truly having the slightest idea. They only see the first layer of the onion, which we allow to slowly strip away. And deep within is a layer of vulnerability that yearns for the true promises of God to manifest.

As a young teen many moons ago, I witnessed many young relationships; to me it seemed as though it were a hookup pandemic. And for a while it did not really bother me. I was completely unfazed. My mindset was more on finishing college, getting a decent job to pay for my travels across the world, and working with children. Trust me, I had an extensive list of things that I was working on, so being in a relationship with a boy was not a priority for me.

Now, we all know the enemy loves to play tag with people we all hold dear to our hearts. And if they are not careful, they unintentionally allow themselves to be used as a puppet for the enemy. And this is also where we as believers in Christ Jesus must remain steadfast and firm in His words, promises, and directions for our walk in Him.

"You know, my love, you are young and beautiful. Why haven't you got a boyfriend yet? You know you aren't getting any younger. And time is flying by. You really should start looking for a boyfriend before it's too late."

"Well," I said, "I am actually leaving that all to God, because He truly knows the desires of my heart, and in His perfect timing, He will lead me to the one He has for me or Him to me."

"Oh no, there is no such thing as a perfect man. And you can't wait on God for them. You can choose from the ones you see."

Upon hearing this individual try to give me such a worthless advice that I did not ask for and did not need, it enraged me from within my spirit. And without warning of self-control, I spoke with such authority. "Look, I did not ask you for your advice, nor do I need it. Your opinion to me does not matter because I do not pray to you, and you did not die for my sins. So you can take your opinion and stick it where the sun doesn't shine. If God says He has the perfect one for me, then I believe Him. My personal life is none of your business. Now you have yourself a blessed day."

As speechless as she was, quietly she indeed walked away. This individual had kids my age also, and I wondered if that was the same stupid advice, she gave her daughters. Many of you might think that was a rude response, and others might think that was the perfect response. However, whether you agree or disagree, keep in mind I was still a child, better yet, in my mid-teens, learning more about who God was and who I was in Him, furthermore, discovering the wonders of trusting His directions and instructions for my life.

There are so many of us who live 24/7 in the house of the Lord and yet still lack the basic wisdom and knowledge of the Most High God. When one has experienced bad relationships and has not been delivered from the hurt and trauma, it becomes a holding ground for unworthy advice to those who are young and trusting in the perfectwill and spoken word for their lives from God. Their advice can become discouraging and damaging to the young believer's faith.

Now here I was in my quiet moment, and my mind began to ponder on the bad advice suggested to me by this individual. "Was there any truth to it?" I asked myself. Why should it be an issue whether I have a boyfriend at this stage or not? "What was the big deal in dating right now," I asked myself. "Well, maybe it isn't a bad idea to just have one to say I have one, right?"

"Okay, if a nice-looking guy asks me out, I will consider it," I said to myself. Friends, it truly is not okay to be disobedient to God or His directions. Believe it or not, He really does know what's best for our lives; after all, He is the one who created us.

Anyway, upon arriving to college. I felt a little strange; everyone walking past was smiling and greeting me and, calling me by my name. "How in the world do they all know my name?" I said to myself. As I got to the middle of the corridor, I saw this huge standing poster of myself with a message: "Our New Student President." Suddenly, I wanted to find a secret place to hide and find out who in their right mind would do something like this.

I tried to keep a smile on my face as if I knew about this. And making my way to lecture, I saw my lecturer, and then she began to congratulate me. But seeing the confused and troubling look on my face, she began to explain how all of that transpired. There was an internal review of a few selected student names placed forward, and my name was in the mix. Herself included voted for me to become the next student president, and I had gotten most votes from the board. And after the votes passed the board, they put it forward to all the staff and students at the college to finally vote, upon which I received majority of the votes.

After hearing all of that, I was speechless. That evening I went home asking myself what exactly they saw in me that would cause them to make such a decision. I mean, I saw myself more of an introvert than out extrovert. Moreover, I enjoy helping behind the scenes and not in the spotlight. After a week, I eventually gave in and try getting used to seeing my face everywhere around the college, most of all, getting used to a lot of fellow students feeling at ease to approach and sit with me during lunch and their free time.

There was one fellow student who I was always seeing and greeting me, but never stopped to have a conversation. Sure enough, he plucked up the courage to sit by me and struck up a conversation. After a few months of friendship and email conversations and seeing each other in college and on the same bus, he built up the courage to ask me out on a date, and that was when I was more convinced to exchange phone numbers. I believe that was the day he felt a breakthrough of finally getting my phone number after months and months of trying to convince me to.

We went on the first date, and it went well. We had a good friendship, so nothing was awkward. After about two weeks had passed, I explained how important it was to me that he worked on his relationship with God. Yes, he had one, but it was not a priority, and it really bothered me within. Even though he was this great and gentle soul, my spirit could not be at peace.

Finally, I had a free weekend from all my testing and assessments. I agreed to go with him to the theater and then dinner. But during the movie, the Holy Spirit said to me, "You must break it off with him. He is not the one God has for you." Yep, there goes God popping my tiny bubble of what-ifs and maybes. I really did not want to acknowledge what the Holy Spirit had revealed to me. I needed time to think alone, so I tried my best to keep a smile on my face. However, he still noticed I seemed a bit worried, which I tried to dismiss.

I could not help but notice how service on Sunday was hot and spicy. Our pastor was on fire with the Word of God. It was not the message he had prepared to share. Somehow the service got shifted, as he closed his notebook and asked one of the ushers to take the stand away. After a few moments of complete silence, he began to share an encounter he had with God, instructing him, which led him directly to his wife who God had for him.

Somehow, I began to feel as though God was trying to get my attention. Then our pastor said, "Let's read the Word of God, go to 2 Corinthians 6:14." In that moment I knew God was speaking to me and reminding me of His words. I began to feel convicted and disappointed with myself. "Do not be unequally yoked together with unbelievers. For what fellowship has righteousness with lawlessness? And what communion has light with darkness? Do not take my word for it, please. I encourage you to read it for yourselves and ask God for wisdom in this situation. I know that this is a word for someone; just remember God knows exactly what He is doing, so trust Him." As he finished and began to pray, I could not help but felt as though I had just gotten an ear bashing and a butt-whooping.

I knew what I had to do; however, I was trying to negotiate with God. That Sunday afternoon I went home and read the entire chapter over and over, and nothing changed. None of my excuses could match the will and direction of the Lord. His words were final and no matter what, I had to be obedient one way or another.

I am sure that I am not the only believer who has often tried to negotiate with the Word and will of God in their lives. What makes us think we can ever negotiate with the Almighty God? Are we not the creation and He the creator? How dare we try to negotiate with Him like we do our earthly parents, believing we can manipulate Him like we do them to get our own way. When did we become so arrogant in our own ways? Do we think we can help Him lead us to live a righteous life in His divine grace?

My flesh said, "God how do you expect me to break up with him? I can try and get him to come to church more often, and I can also share the Word with him." My spirit said, "Well, He did tell you not to date. And you still went ahead, knowing that he is not the one God said He has for you. Obedience is better than sacrifice." The question now is, when would be the best time to break it off with this guy. And furthermore, how heartbroken he will be, as much as I already like him, and he really likes me? "Lord, can you not allow him to end things rather than have me do it?" I asked, not getting a reply from God.

When we find ourselves in situations like this and others, please go back and recall the last instruction our Heavenly Father instructed you to do. This will help so much in the long run for us not having to blame others for our own decisions and mistakes. And even more so, complain about how God can allow this and that to happen, when in fact, we are weeping the repercussions of our actions and disobedience to His will.

Now, when you come to the end of your rope and exhausted all your wild ideas and knowledge on how you know best, surrender, surrender it all to our Heavenly Father and repent. Release it all in His hands and start again, but this time allowing God to lead and direct your every path within every aspect of your life, no matter how big or how small the decisions are, and believe me, you will witness the difference between doing things your way and God's way.

Our ways bring confusion, distraction, dead-ends, drought, deceitfulness, self-denial, and a lack of godly knowledge, whereas doing things in the will of God will lead to a lifetime of blessings, not just for you but also for the generations that will be allowed to birth out of you. Blessings of His perfect peace, blessings of protection amid chaos around you and your family. Remember, the riches of God can never be measured by the riches of this world. God's blessings and riches can never be counted nor measured by man or man's standards.

The riches from God in your life will never just be for you and your household alone. You do not have enough room to contain it all. And that is why we must remain like a tunnel for it to flow through. Because that is how we allow ourselves to be used by God, and even though the blessing flows through us, we are also experiencing the blessing.

Talk about compromising with the Word and will of God in and over your life. By no means should this ever be an option, no matter how good it looks or how great it may sound at the time. Compromising the will and Word of God in your life will always delay your blessings, the other persons' blessings, not to mention the hurt you may cause them, or they may cause you in the long run.

> Do not be unequally yoked together with unbelievers. For what fellowship has righteousness with lawlessness? And what communion has light with darkness? And what accord has Christ with Belial? Or what part has a believer with an unbeliever? And what agreement has the temple of God with idols? For you are the temple of the living God. As God has said: "I will dwell in them and walk among them. I will be their God, and they shall be My people.
>
> —2 Corinthians 6:14–16

You and I can make all the excuses we want; however, at the end of the day we cannot change the will of God nor the Word of God over our lives. For example, the will of God was for the people of Nineveh to hear His words and take heed of them. However, the messenger whom God had chosen to deliver it had other thoughts and ideas of why he should not speak the Word of God and be obedient. Thus, he tried to venture out in a totally different direction (Jonah 1,2,3). His disregards and disobedience still did not deter the Word of God or His divine plans. Believe it or not, God really does know our beginning and our ends, so we can never outrun from God or hide from His Presence. (seePs 139)

> For as the rain and snow come down from heaven, and do not return there without watering the earth, making it bear and sprout, and providing seed to the Sower and bread to the eater, So will My word be which goes out of My mouth; It will not return to Me void Without accomplishing what I desire, And without succeeding in the matter for which I sent it.
> —Isaiah 55:10–11

I remember when I was little, growing up back in the Caribbean. I don't know about you, but our old folks back in Sunday school made sure to teach us in such a way that it remains with us as adults. They gave us the short version of the chapter from the scriptures that kind of sums up what the story was about. And you know, it was with the tambourines and clapping our hands.

Song: "Adam in the garden hidin', hidin', hidin'
   Adam in the garden hidin', hidin' himself from God
   Adam, where art thou, Adam where art thou
   Adam hide himself from God."

I chuckle, because as simple as the song may sound, the story and lesson behind it is immensely powerful and applies to our daily struggles and walk with God. The song was based on Genesis 3:8. Playing hide and seek with God is a waste of time because you are only trying to fool yourself in the end. There is nowhere we could place ourselves where God would not be right there for us to call on, lean on, and surrender to. Nowhere! (Ps. 139:7–12).

This is why it is vitally important that we not only allow the Holy Spirit to teach us, but also seek the word of God for ourselves so that we are not deceived by words or emotions from fellow believers or the enemy. Look at it this way, if you are doing some gardening or even just planting a few seeds of flowers, you prepare the soil and make sure it is not dry, and you do all you need to and plant your seed and then water it and place it in the best position for the sunlight to shine on it. But here comes someone who does not like the way you planted your flowers and does not believe they will grow in the way you have established it to. So, they try to clip bits of it and choke it with extra soil with poison in its mixture. Now, as the gardener, how would that cause you to feel?

The ways of the Lord are perfect. His handiwork is matchless. His words are perfect. His will is perfect. His directions may feel somewhat challenging to us, but they are perfectly rewarding and faith-building.

So, if anyone was trying to contradict what God has said to me and/or was leading me to, I would be extremely defensive and would speak up. However, in that moment it felt as though I was rebuking a discouraging spirit from someone who was more seasonal in their faith, or so I thought, and who also should have known better.

> Don't overlook the obvious here, friends. With God, one day is as good as a thousand years, a thousand years as a day. God isn't late with his promise as some measure lateness. He is restraining himself on account of you, holding back the End because he doesn't want anyone lost. He's giving everyone space and time to change.
>
> —2 Peter 3:8–9, MSG

You can never fully begin something new without finishing first what God has called you to complete to move forward. Jonah tried to go the opposite of where God sent him and still ended up right back at the beginning. My dear friends, it does not matter where we try to run to or how long we try to run for, the will and Word of God in and over our lives remains the same. The only difference there might be is the timing in which it will come to pass.

We must learn to recognize our fears as they are developing. And bring then under the full submission of God so, that we may not become blindsided with the deceptions of the enemy. But allowing our faith in God to captivate the truth of who we are in Him and who He has called us to be and do. Who God says that we are is far more important than what man says or try to make use believe we are. We are the apple of God's eye and in Him there are no fears, no doubts, what ifs, buts or maybes. There are so many others in the Bible who had to surrender to the will of the Almighty, even when they thought they knew better than Him. There are times when we children of the Most High still behave like this and then wonder why doors of breakthrough have not been opened. Moreover, we find ourselves stuck going around and round in a cycle. Could this be because we think more of others, so we believe more in them and over them than we do for ourselves? The same strength we use to encourage others is the strength we ought to use and encourage ourselves. We cannot preach one thing and not practice it; otherwise, wouldn't we be hypocritical? Why do we have faith for others but struggle to have faith for ourselves?

Is it because we do not believe we are good enough?

I would like to believe that we all struggle with this. Sometimes we unconsciously choose to listen to the lies whispered in our ears from the enemy that we are not good enough or that we shall never be good enough. What makes you so special? Look what you have done in the past; you can never recover from that. Look how many times you have sinned and turned your back on God. Have you ever noticed that the enemy never fails to remind us of our past mistakes and tries to cripple us in such a way that our emotions attach to all the lies? And yet he can never address our future to us.

The moment we take our eyes off the Lord and get distracted by the antics of the enemy is when we lose total sight of the light and truth of God. We cannot allow the voice of the enemy to overshadow or silence or drown out and destroy our relationship with our Heavenly Father by believing his lies over what God has spoken.

Look at it this way: the enemy will never cheer you on to finish your race and cross the finish line successfully. He will always remind you of how ugly you are running; he will boo you and shout all manner of things to break your spirit and your attention. However, on the other hand, God will always cheer you on, even when fear creeps in, when doubt is knocking on the windows of your heart. He reminds us that He is right there running with us, "Just a little further! You are almost there. Don't give up! We are in this together."

The enemy pulls you back and discourages you not to believe, but God pushes you forward and encourages you to believe! When we doubt the Word of God in our lives, we are not only compromising our trust and faith in Him but in who He created us to be. And this can be an extremely dangerous path to venture on, a path that was never created for us to experience, which could result in the enemy taking us for a physical and emotional roller coaster ride to destruction.

My friends, we must never allow our fears to overshadow our faith and trust in God. Our fears put limits on our faith to genuinely believe and do not know our strength, but our faith knows the impossibilities are more than possible and has no limits on believing above and beyond the limits of expectations we are often surrounded by and must face.

We must begin to believe God's plan for our future and not the enemy's facts of our past. Remember, we no longer live in our past. It is behind us; we do not live in yesterday. We are living in the now, in the present, in God's Presence. We are not who we used to be. Our mistakes do not define us, but rather refine us. We are renewed in the Almighty, the God of Abraham, Isaac, and Jacob.

In our everyday life in some respects, have you noticed we share similarities with the story of the prodigal son? It may not be as vast as the story in the Bible but is still subtle in such a way that we dismiss it or rather dismiss the daily voice of God in our lives. Let me ask, is our attention on His divine directions or is it on the next quick fix shortcut that looks as though it is saving us time and money by cutting off our life support system of faith in Him?

Why do we believe the lies of the enemy, thinking we can go about doing it ourselves? Why are we allowing ourselves to continue believe such a lie? How many scars and bruises are marked on us reminding us that it almost cost us our lives? God had to step in to rescue us.

What is much sweeter than God's divine Presence? What is more exciting than the plan and purpose that God has for our future? Is life so enjoyable outside the will and protection of God? Is it everlasting, is it peaceful, is it love, is it living, or is it just existing to a dead end?

Have you ever heard the saying "The grass is greener on the other side"? But a wise person would reply, "Well, the grass isn't greener on the other side, it's only greener wherever you water it."

The enemy will always use the facts of your past to tempt you. He is not new nor are his tactics; they are old and outdated and dusty. So, he takes an old tray, dusts it off a bit, and dresses it up with a few pieces of this and that to make it look colorful and brand new. Its's like taking old rusty bang-up parts from a junk yard of cars and try to well the pieces together to pass off and sell as an Aston Martin DB12 when in real fact it is a makeshift junk yard scrap painted and welled up together over to make you believe otherwise. We ought to stop allowing ourselves to believe the lies and giving attention to these makeshift shortcut microwave blessings to try catch up with our neighbors, friends and pressure society tries to push on us.

If we do not know our own values and worth or purpose in God, we will easily lose sight and fall for these things.

"God, I know you said wait, but look, she looks so cute in the way she talks, the way she carries herself. She's got it all together, and we have so much in common. I am just going to hang out for a bit with her. She is always showing up where I am and doing things for me." "But God, he looks so sharp and on point. His tapeline is slick. How can You tell me no to him. He gives me all the attention, and he is always complimenting me and making me laugh. Everyone loves him and he is so polite." Or better yet, "God, I know you said You have that one for me, but You are taking too long, so I went ahead of You and think I found one better that I can start courting now."

How many times have we gone there and still dismissed the Word of God over and through our lives because of what is being presented before us that we can just reach and touch with our hands? It is like Samson putting his hand in the dead carcass of the lion and reaching for the honey, eating it as though eating from the forbidden tree like Adam and Eve (Judg. 14, Lev. 11).

The enemy will always lie to us and try to get us to believe there is a better life than what God has for us because He takes too long in our minds, and he can give it to you right here and right now.

When was it a terrible idea to wait on God? Has He ever been late? When we stand on the platform awaiting the train to a destination, on the display board it informs us of how long we must wait. Can you jump on the empty track and walk the journey, or do you wait safely for the train to pull up and take you? Likewise, we ought to use the wisdom from the Spirit of God and wait.

The most dangerous place that we could ever position ourselves is out from under the safety and protection of God. Once we remove ourselves from His protection, we then find ourselves in the playground of the enemy.

And just like the prodigal son (Luke 15:11–32), instead of remaining in his Father's presence and will, he had other plans and believed that what he had was enough to sustain him in the world without his father. This is the perfect picture of how we are with the Lord, our God, the Most High. Because we feel as though our well is full enough and His grace is sufficient to forgive us as we venture out on our own trying to do life as we witness the world does part taking and compromising ourselves, sounding, looking, and dressing as the world. How can we ever be set apart and be ambassadors for the Kingdom of God if we are not carrying ourselves in His likeness? How then can we be light bearers for the lost and broken? If our light is shining identically to a broken world what hope is there? If the runway lights for the plane to land shine like the lights in Las Vegas strips where the parties come alive, could that aircraft find its way to land safely or would the pilot get confused? (Matt 5:14-16)

The prodigal son did it all and tried it all, but then his well began to dry up. Like him, we too become physically and spiritually dry and dead. We need to get up and dust ourselves off, lift up our heads and come alive. We need to remember and go back to our first love, our Heavenly Father and King. We too must return to the living water of our souls. The one of whom we tasted and saw was good. The one of whom we took our eyes off and turned our backs on, and yet still He never forsake us as we were being unfaithful to Him.

When rock bottom came, look where the prodigal son found himself. He was feeding pigs and was so low to the point he would also eat that which the pigs ate too. Even though his father had more than the provision, he thought he knew better. And by his own decision, here he was regretting his actions. You can say the grass was not so greener on the other side after all.

If only he had remained and be obedient. The result of his disobedience was not as he had envisioned it to be. However, we could say even though he was humiliated, he was also humbled and brought to humility by learning from his mistakes. Yet how many of us are also guilty of this disobedience to our Heavenly Father? How many of us have tried to take a shortcut toward the finish line but end up going right back to where God has started us from in the race? Or how many times did He have to reset the race with you? How many times have we been humbled by His truth, words, and wisdom in and over our lives? There are some of us wanting to cross the finish line without putting in the leg work and build up those muscles. I know that we are all guilty of this in our journey and relationship with the Lord.

Your faith is your hope and your hope is your anchor which holds you grounded in Him, His word and His will. Whatever you may be facing, thinking, or doing do not lose your hope in God, do not trade it, and most importantly do not give up.

Enough

◇◇

Y ou and I are good enough!
You and I are enough for the plans of God to use.
Society may dismiss you and I and overlook us, but the Almighty God has not.
We are exactly who He has sought out and has called.
Read Psalm 139:13–14.

Prayer: Prince of Peace

Merciful Father, Prince of peace, we just want to thank You for Your loving-kindness. Your grace and mercy are everlasting to everlasting and have no limits for us. Please forgive us for all the things we have made it to be, forgive us for always trying to do things with our own strength and knowledge. Forgive us for pushing aside Your Word and truth because we allow our emotions to take control over our spirit. Forgive us for turning our backs on You when You call us to repentance. Forgive us, Father, forgive us for not putting You first in our daily walk and acknowledge You in all that we do and speak. Forgive us for not walking in right standing with our neighbors. Forgive us and lead us back to the heart of true worship with You where it is all about You. Lead us back to Your loving arms of grace of love, heal and renew our hearts, and restore our minds from all the lies of the enemy as we recommit and surrender all to You. Help us to believe again, help us to hope again, as we continue to long and yarn for You and Your Presence. In Jesus's Mighty name we pray. Amen.

A Journey beyond a Journey

◇◇

> But when he came to himself, he said, 'How many of my father's hired servants have bread enough and to spare, and I perish with hunger! I will arise and go to my father, and will say to him, "Father, I have sinned against heaven and before you, and I am no longer worthy to be called your son. Make me like one of your hired servants.
>
> —Luke 15:17–19

This journey beyond a journey has not been an easy one. And I do not believe it was supposed to be, either. Physically, spiritually, and emotionally what I thought I knew about God has had me stretched in ways I could have never imagined; the hills, the valleys, and the rivers that I never envisioned I would learn to climb, to sit in, and learn how to swim.

When God truly calls you out into the deep, I can see now that it is to teach you to lean on Him only, to trust Him only, and for Him to teach you more about His plan and purpose for your life.

He takes you out into the deep, empties you of all the foolishness of man, and reshapes and molds you from the inside out for you to truly be reborn in His likeness. I have come across a lot of individuals who have said to me, "My dear, you have to trust the process; it comes with the journey because it is what helps build your character in Him." Honestly speaking, when I first heard it, I wanted to slap them and tell them, "Well, why don't you walk in my shoes for a day and then repeat that to yourself?"

After fighting and fighting with God, you then find yourself surrendering little by little to Him, as He begins to strip away all the barricades of walls you had put up to protect yourself. And as He begins to tear down these makeshift walls of protection, you begin to see how vulnerable and alone you are without Him. As you allow this vulnerable part of your heart to solely surrender into His arms of grace and learn how to truly trust Him, you not only find yourself but also find your identity in Him.

Your walk, your talk, your confidence, your dance, your worship, your joy, and your light begin to shine differently with His covering over you. When I think about this journey and where God started me from, what He brought me through and to where He has me right now, tears flow down my cheeks in awe of Him and His never-ending love and grace for me.

I have lost so much and so many, yet He has allowed me to gain what is truly needed, and I am so thankful. There have been times where I almost gave up, and there were times my faith in Him was deeply tried, tested and placed in the fiery furnace, but God still remained true. Never once did He leave me alone, never once did He fail to sit with me when I could not stand, and never once did He not increase His strength in me to raise my hands in worship to Him. Never once has God turned His back on me when I found myself in doubt and the waves and wind wanted to drown me. He reminded me to look up, look up to the hills from where my help had always come from, and that was Him.

Never once did He not wipe the tears from my eyes as I cried myself to sleep while resting in His presence. My dear friends there is nothing that is more precious than having a personal relationship with God. A life without God is not a life living in the fullness of who you were created to be and love.

Living a life without a godly purpose is like trying to drive a car without an engine. The car and you cannot move without knowing your purpose in God, and having the right tools and parts. You will just be stuck like a rock as time and seasons passes you by with the different elements covering you until you are buried with sorrows and regrets.

You are more than your past failures and mistakes; it was your training ground. From there you grew and got stronger and wiser with the knowledge of God, even though at times the training ground felt more like a battlefield. The enemies encamped around you could not take you out because God was and is always with you.

> He will not allow your foot to slip; He who watches over you will not slumber. Behold, He who watches over Israel will neither slumber nor sleep. The Lord is your protector; The Lord is your shade on your right hand. The sun will not beat down on you by day, nor the moon by night. The Lord will protect you from all evil; He will keep your soul. The Lord will guard your going out and your coming in.
>
> —Psalm 121:3–8

Being on this journey beyond a journey has not only opened my eyes to the various aspects of being a follower and believer of Yeshua. Seeing others as they choose to live with and without Him, I can honestly say this walk stretched me beyond anything I could have ever imagined.

Yes, at times I do get a little scared of the unknown while I still hold on to my hope, which is my anchor in Him, to guide me through the dark patches of the tunnels and valleys and hill tops and oceans deep. Sometimes I do wonder when He is silent if I am on His mind or if I have steered out of His view, but we know this is never true and is just a smoke screen from the defeated one.

Often, I do wonder about His promises to me, and sometimes I hear myself trying to question the timing of when He might fulfill them. And then I am reminded of my task at hand that needs to be completed. As subtle as it is, we do not realize that we try to negotiate with God and the blessings that He has in store for us. We cannot negotiate with the Almighty God.

So, it is in our best spiritual and physical interest to take heed of the Word and instruction of God's will and purpose in our lives.

I thought this journey would have been the most difficult and trying of my faith. It was not a piece of chocolate cake. It required a lot of sacrifices, bringing your flesh under submission to the Spirit of God, surrendering wholeheartedly, and allowing Him to strip away every layer to the very core. In return, He healed and enlarged my heart and filled it with such an unfathomable, unconditional love and humility.

Letting go is never easy, but it sure is worth it.

> My brethren, count it all joy when you fall into various trials, knowing that the testing of your faith produces patience. But let patience have its perfect work, that you may be perfect and complete, lacking nothing. If any of you lacks wisdom, let him ask of God, who gives to all liberally and without reproach, and it will be given to him.
>
> —James 1:2–5

This journey beyond a journey with God allowed me to learn the importance of being forgiven and to also forgive, to be healed and how to pray for healing, how to love and be loved, and how to take the leap of faith with God even when I cannot see the ending or have glimpsed the blueprint of the next chapter.

Even though it may have taken a long time, God's unconditional love was rooted within me and has set me free from the lies, fears of shame, rejection, and not believing that I am enough.

This journey was not just a physical walking lesson but a spiritual and intimate walk with God.

Faith is a season journeyed; our testimonies are birthed from our journey of faith walked with God.

A Continuous Journey

There will always be a few things along our journey with God that we will regret; however, we must not dwell on it and allow those things to fester and take refuge in our hearts. It would not be healthy for our hearts or our spirits and would give the enemy a front row seat to torment us. Rather, we ought to learn from our mistakes and move forward, testifying to the goodness of God in our lives. After all, it is hearing the Word of God that increases our faith in Him. And if someone else is testifying to His goodness in their lives, we too can use that as a stepping stone to go to Him and try Him for ourselves.

My journey continues…

Secret for The Journey

The secret to life's journey is do it with God.
Keep on going when it is rough and tough.
Keep on going when the crowdss are against you, they were against Jesus too.
Keep on going when walking is too painful.
Keep on going when standing becomes unbearable.
Remember, before you learnt how to walk you crawled.
Before you learnt how to balance and stand, you were kneeling.
Keep on going when all you have left is Jesus.
He is your compass through life's journey.
He is in the beginning with you.
He is in the middle with you.
And He is crossing the finish line with you.
A Journey beyond a journey.
Yet another thing I observed under the sun is that the races aren't won by the swift of battles by the strong, and that food doesn't go to the wise or wealth to the intelligent or favor to the experts; rather, time and chance rule them all. Ecc 9:11 CJB
My Journey is My Obedience.